DISCARD

THE STORY OF
AMERICA'S
TUNNELS

· CONNECTING · A · CONTINENT ·

THE STORY OF
AMERICA'S
TUNNELS

**Ray Spangenburg
and Diane K. Moser**

Heritage Middle School
Middlebury, IN. 46540

8355

Facts On File
New York • Oxford

The Story of America's Tunnels

Copyright © 1993 by Ray Spangenburg and Diane K. Moser

All rights reserved. No part of this book may be reproduced or utilized in any form or by any means, electronic or mechanical, including photocopying, recording, or by any information storage or retrieval systems, without permission in writing from the publisher. For information contact:

Facts On File, Inc.
460 Park Avenue South
New York NY 10016
USA

Facts On File Limited
c/o Roundhouse Publishing Ltd.
P.O. Box 140
Oxford OX2 7SF
United Kingdom

Library of Congress Cataloging-in-Publication Data
Spangenburg, Ray, 1939–
The story of America's tunnels / Ray Spangenburg and Diane Moser.
p. cm. — (Connecting a continent)
Includes bibliographical references and index.
Summary: Traces the history of tunnel-building in America,
from the earliest days of the Schuylkill Navigation Tunnel to the complex
technology of today's immersed-tube tunnels.
ISBN 0-8160-2258-5
1. Tunnels—United States—Juvenile literature. 2. Tunneling—
United States—Juvenile literature. [1. Tunnels. 2. Tunneling.]
I. Moser, Diane, 1944– . II. Title. III. Series: Spangenburg,
Ray, 1939– Connecting a continent.
TA807.S62   1992
624.1′93′0973—dc20   92-17313

British CIP data available on request from the British Library.

Facts On File books are available at special discounts when purchased in bulk quantities for businesses, associations, institutions or sales promotions. Please contact our Special Sales Department in New York at 212/683-2244 (dial 800/322-8755 except in NY, AK or HI).

Text and jacket design by Donna Sinisgalli
Composition by Facts On File, Inc.
Manufactured by the Maple-Vail Book Manufacturing Group
Printed in the United States of America

10 9 8 7 6 5 4 3 2 1

This book is printed on acid-free paper.

CONTENTS

To the memory of
Richard Harding Davis
(1864–1916)
whose great stories of wonderful adventures
inspired a generation
of writers, journalists and engineers

ACKNOWLEDGMENTS

We would like to thank the many individuals, too numerous to name, who helped us on this project—we greatly appreciated both their aid and their enthusiasm. Several made special contributions, going out of their way to help make this book better, including: Anne Bennof of the American Association of Railroads; Mary Hanel, formerly of the California Department of Transportation Archives; Richard Hellinger of the New York Transit Museum; Sherry Roberts; Bill Shank of the American Canal and Transportation Center; and William Worthington of the Smithsonian Institution. A special thanks also to Liz Nolley and Nicole Bowen for their thoughtful editing and to James Warren at Facts On File for his many insightful suggestions in shaping this series.

1

DIGGING UNDER AND THROUGH: THE STORY OF EARLY TUNNELING

People have "gone underground" for various reasons for many thousands of years—ever since early humans first used the shelter of natural caves. Even though digging underground caverns and passageways was often hazardous, people began digging artificial caves and tunnels long ago for religious reasons, for burial, for water transport and for military advantage. Going underground provided protection, privacy, secrecy and, in many cases, a shorter (sometimes the only) way to transport water from its source to a town, or to remove sewage from a congested city. Once engineering technology developed enough to make longer tunnels possible, transportation tunnels—the subject of this book—enabled travelers and merchants to take shortcuts through impassable mountains and under rivers and bays.

The story of tunneling since those earliest times is one of adventure and tragedy. It is a story of heroes who used their muscles and courage to dig through the earth. It is also a tale of geologists and engineers who used a growing base of knowledge and technology to learn about the earth they dug through, overcoming safety hazards and meeting the challenges of difficult terrain.

People dug the earliest tunnels—in Paleolithic times (the early Stone Age, about 2 million years ago)—by extending natural tunnels. Later, as metals

began to be used for tools, weapons and trade, they began to devise methods of mining ores from the ground. Ore outcrops, where rock has been pushed up to the surface, provided the first easy access. But probably as far back as 15,000 years ago, people began digging into the ground beneath the outcroppings to find more ores. Digging a vertical hole, known as sinking a shaft, was an early mining technique, followed later by more elaborate galleries (horizontal tunnels) and caverns. Advances in the use of metals and other minerals led in turn to even more interest in further tunneling, and miners and tunnelers looked for ways to improve their methods.

They also found more reasons to tunnel. Recorded history shows that Rameses II built rock temples in ancient Egypt in 1250 B.C., and in India, around the third century B.C., Brahmins and Buddhists built monasteries and temples into the rocks. The ancient Babylonians built tunnels for irrigation. And more than 2,500 years ago, around the 6th century B.C., ancient Greeks carved out a 3,300-foot tunnel to carry water on the island of Samos. The engineer, the first recorded in history by name, was a man named Eupalinus of Megara.

The Romans, whose engineering skills enabled them to link their extensive empire by roads, bridges and aqueducts, were also among the first able tunnelers. They sank vertical shafts from which to drive

1

horizontal tunnels, later using the shafts for ventilation and light. They also devised a method for driving through rock, known as fire-quenching, which was used for many centuries until more effective blasting and drilling techniques were developed. Probably adapted from the early Etruscans who preceded the Romans in Italy, the technique called for heating the rock to be tunneled until it was red-hot, then throwing water against the rock face. The rock would crack and scale as a result of the sudden change in temperature and then could be chipped away. The Romans cut a 4,800-foot transportation tunnel, known as the Pausilippo Tunnel, through volcanic rock in 36 B.C., providing passage from Pozzuoli to Naples. Perhaps the largest tunnel of ancient times, it was 25 feet wide and 30 feet high, big enough to accommodate the brisk traffic of carts and horses that passed through.

Tunneling was also used by military forces to attack walled cities or to supply cities under siege. Accounts exist of tunneling attackers and countermeasures for defense against them as far back as 214 B.C.

THE CHALLENGE OF THE UNDERGROUND

Building a tunnel is a complex engineering project that calls for extensive information gathering, coordinated decisions, integrated planning and organized execution on a grand scale. The successful completion of the project, the lives of the workers and, in the case of transportation tunnels, the lives of the people who will use the tunnel depend on how carefully the hazardous digging and construction are planned.

Geology plays a key role. Engineers have to know what kind of earth the tunnel will go through. Is it solid hard rock or does it have faults or cracks? Do seams of other types of rock or ground ribbon through it? Or is it soft ground, such as silt, mud, gravel or loose rock? Is it water laden? The earliest tunnelers didn't always have ways for finding the

As late as the 18th century, miners and tunnelers employed the ancient Roman technique of using a bonfire to split rock. Denis Diderot, *L'Encyclopédie,* 1751–72

2

What a Tunneler Needs to Know About Geology Before Beginning to Dig

Probably the biggest danger in tunneling is the possibility of cave-ins. When people first began digging underground, no one knew a lot about geology. But miners and other tunnelers soon discovered, from grim and tragic accidents, that even what appeared to be solid rock could shift and collapse when its underlying supports were removed.

Tunneling falls into two basic types—digging through hard rock (which forms a natural arch but is hard to penetrate) and digging through soft ground, clay or water-laden ground (which caves in easily).

Homogeneous hard rock (rock of one consistent type) forms a natural arch, and tunneling through it presents few hazards if the tunneler takes care to disturb the rock's natural strength as little as possible. A semi-elliptical arch across the top of the tunnel will keep the vault from collapsing, no matter how deep the tunnel. But few tunnelers outside Scandinavia and Canada have met with the good luck to encounter this type of rock.

Usually, the rock to be tunneled has fissures or the ground is soft—a chalky stone or clay or silt or shale. Fissures in rock that looks otherwise solid can bisect layers so that, when supporting rock beneath is removed, the rock has no continuity and falls. When a tunnel cuts through two types of rock laying side by side, at the point where the digging moves across the juncture, a collapse is very likely. Sometimes water percolating through a mass of rock will leave deposits of foreign material, which, if encountered in tunneling, will lose their cohesion and spill into the excavation.

If these problems occur on a large enough scale, the consequences to the tunnel and those working in it can be disastrous. Stop-gap measures—such as extra bracing or a break-dam across a cavity—may sufficiently strengthen the structure and can sometimes stop the spills and save a tunnel. Firm ground—some clays, shale, and cemented sands—can be trusted to hold long enough for timbers to be placed after excavation is complete. But for softer ground—damp sand, soft earth, squeezing clay—the ground must be held back while the digging is done, and then also later, once the tunnel is complete.

answers to these questions—nor did they often even think of them. Today, however, no tunnel is begun without a thorough survey of the surrounding ground.

Decisions must be made about excavation methods—based on available tools and the demands of the terrain. Will the tunnel be dug full face—removing the entire bore all at once? Or will it be done in sections, and if so in what order? Early tunnelers used a variety of systems for carving out tunnels—often depending on the combination of ground types through which they were driving. The Egyptians dug tunnels deep into the cliffs of the Nile—probably using what is now known as the center core method. A hole large enough for a man to work in was cut beneath the future roof of the tunnel, then ditches were extended down the walls on both sides, leaving a platform in the middle. Finally, the center core was

removed, slab by slab, for use in building. To create a slab, a groove was cut, about 4 inches wide. Wedges were then worked into the groove. In soft rock, wooden wedges soaked in water would swell enough to split the rock. Similar methods, with improvements and variations, were later developed and adapted for larger excavations, different types of rock, and tunnels for different purposes. Elaborate sequences of excavation, combined with complex timbering, would later be conceived in attempts to prevent cave-ins. And new technology always found its way into tunneling methods as it was invented.

But the challenges of tunneling don't end with settling on an excavation method. Transportation from the tunnel face to the surface presents yet another problem. How will materials and supplies be transported to the sandhogs (the workers who dig the tunnel) and how will the excavated material be car-

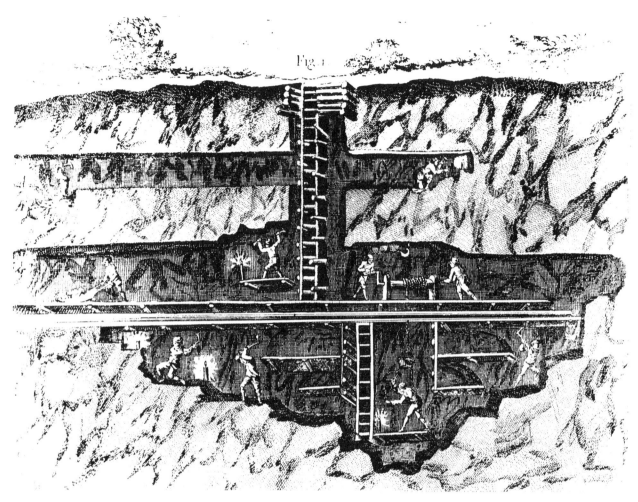

Tunneling and mining techniques used by the ancients lasted well into the 18th century. Workers dug in cramped, dank quarters, breathing bad air and using awkward digging techniques, crude tools and rudimentary hoists. The work was both back-breaking and dangerous, lit only by dim torches. Denis Diderot, *L'Encyclopédie,* 1751–72

ried out? How will the workers come and go? And by what route? Will a shaft be used, or a parallel heading (or smaller tunnel), or can the main bore be used?

What provision will be made for preventing cave-ins? Will framing and bracing be needed? Will it be necessary to build a wall or shell around the tunnel bore to prevent cave-ins? Early tunnelers, who usually took advantage of the natural arch formed by solid rock, faced far fewer problems than later tunnelers who began to drive through soft, irregular ground and, still more recently, took on the ultimate challenge of building tunnels under water.

The environment also has to be livable for workers inside the tunnel. How will the atmosphere deep inside the earth be kept breathable for the workers? Can shafts be sunk for ventilation? Or parallel air ducts? How can working conditions be kept tolerable as the temperature rises above 100°F deep underground?

These are only a few of the questions a tunneler needs to answer before the first shovelful of dirt is turned and the job of tunneling begins. Often, though, as we will see in tracing the saga of America's tunnels, these decisions have to be made on the spot. As emergencies and crises arise and as unexpected problems occur, the creative energy and vigor of those who drive tunnels through rock, mud and silt continue to be put to the test.

2

AMERICA'S FIRST TUNNELS: TAKING THE CANAL BOATS THROUGH

In early America, transportation systems of all kinds grew slowly at first. Native Americans relied primarily on footpaths and natural waterways for transportation—to go on hunting forays or trading expeditions, to stage attacks and defenses against enemies, or to move from place to place. And the colonial settlers from Europe and England who established their first settlements in the 17th century followed their example. They traveled by boats on the rivers or used slightly improved trails and roads and were not quick to build either bridges or tunnels at first.

But America soon became a nation greatly in need of transportation. A vast expanse of usable land extended endlessly, it seemed, to the west. New opportunities, new dreams and new lands to be conquered beckoned, offering new possibilities for a better way of life. As adventurous settlers opened up these areas, the commercial minded recognized a growing trade opportunity—the need for supplies and manufactured goods from the ports and factories of the East.

As a result, some roads were built and improved but, for the most part, they remained rough and primitive. Early wagon traffic was slow and costly. Instead, the waterways along the Atlantic seaboard continued to be America's greatest transportation resource—the great Atlantic Ocean, a coast lacerated with deep bays (such as Boston Harbor, Chesapeake Bay and New York Harbor), a network of navigable

rivers (such as the Potomac, the Hudson, the Delaware and dozens of others), and a countryside dotted with lakes (including the Great Lakes, Lake Champlain and others). Visionaries quickly saw that by connecting these waterways with canals, a great shipping system could be built, free of costly, time-consuming portages. In fact, between 1790 and 1840 over 4,400 miles of canals were constructed in America, although, of those completed before 1825, most were very short. Canals were, however, the sites of the very first transportation tunnels built in America. But it turned out that canals were not the transportation cure-all they seemed at first—a realization that came to light after many were built.

By 1790 there were nearly 30 different canal companies incorporated throughout eight of the original 13 colonies. Many of these were simple navigational improvements circumnavigating falls or rapids along existing waterways—such as the 2-mile Hadley Falls Canal and the 27-mile Middlesex Canal in Massachusetts, the James River Canal in Virginia, and the 22-mile Santee Canal in South Carolina. The great exception was the Erie Canal, the longest canal built during this period. The Erie extended 363 miles and was built between 1817 and 1825 to connect Albany, New York, on the Hudson with Buffalo, New York, on Lake Erie.

It was during this great canal-building hey-day that the first tunnel of any kind was built in the United

Early Canal Tunnels in the United States

1821–1832

DATE	TUNNEL	LENGTH
1821	Schuylkill Navigation Tunnel The first U.S. tunnel begun in 1818; located near Auburn on the Schuylkill Navigation Canal in Pennsylvania	450 ft.
1826	Lebanon Tunnel On the Union Canal near Lebanon, Pennsylvania; begun in 1824	729 ft.
1830	Western Division Canal Tunnel The third tunnel built for any purpose in the United States; enabled the Western Division of Pennsylvania's "Main Line" system to avoid a meandering loop of the Conemaugh River east of Tunnelton, Pennsylvania	850 ft.
1832	Grant's Hill Tunnel At Pittsburgh on the canal extension of the Pennsylvania "Main Line" from the Allegheny River to the Monongahela River; used mostly as a spillway because the connection from the river to the Chesapeake and Ohio Canal was never completed	810 ft.

States. Not surprisingly, it was built for a canal—the Schuylkill Navigation Canal in Pennsylvania.

Building a tunnel for a canal was not a new idea. As far back as the late 17th century in southern France, on the Languedoc Canal, an engineer named Pierre-Paul Riquet became the first to drive a tunnel for a canal. At the time, as tunnel historian Gösta Sandstrom wrote, "such an outrageous solution to a topographical obstruction had never been tried previously." Using gunpowder, possibly for the first time in tunnel building, Riquet's workers blasted a hole 515 feet long, 22 feet wide and 27 feet high through the soft limestone. They drilled holes in the rock, loaded them with black gunpowder, then tamped it down with pegs of wood and detonated, creating a shower of flying rock. The Malpas Tunnel of the Languedoc Canal was completed in 1681.

By the mid-18th century in England, canals had begun to lace the countryside, and tunneling through a hillside was often cheaper than digging an open-air cut deep enough for passage of the waterway. As would also later become the case in the United States, British canals were usually built on a small budget, and narrow canal tunnels became common. Most were originally built without towpaths, and boats were pro-

pelled through by hand. Usually boat workers either pulled a barge through using chains attached to the walls, or poled it through using notches built into the walls for that purpose, or, often, they "legged" through. "Leggers" would lie at the bow of the boat on their backs, extending their legs to the tunnel walls. Then they would take turns pushing against the walls with their feet, propelling the boat forward, as it zigzagged from side to side through the tunnel. It was no easy task. In the 3-mile-long Standedge Tunnel it took leggers 80 minutes to leg a barge through.

In the United States, though, because most canals were so short, none built before 1815 required tunnels.

The Schuylkill Navigation Canal, however, was more ambitious. Originally, the State of Pennsylvania had chartered two companies in 1792 to complete an extensive waterway across the southeastern corner of the state. The plan called for building canals and improving river routes to form inland connections in a great arc from the Susquehanna River, through Reading and down the Schuylkill River to Philadelphia on the Delaware River, a total distance of some 100 miles (farther, actually, as the meandering waterways would travel).

When finished, the Schuylkill Navigation Canal combined 62 miles of canal with 46 miles of improved river navigation pools to stretch 108 miles from Port Carbon, in the coal-laden hills near Pottsville in central Pennsylvania, to Philadelphia. For boats headed into the hills, 92 locks were required to climb a total of 588 feet.

On this canal, near the town of Auburn, the Schuylkill Navigation Company drove the first tunnel in the United States, completed in 1821. Strangely enough, the tunnel could easily have been avoided by rerouting the canal only a few hundred feet west, to another part of the ridge it cut through. But the canal's builders knew how impressive their advertising would sound if they could lay claim to building the nation's first tunnel. So the canal owners elected to punch a 450-foot tunnel through the hill's red shale stone. Workers built a masonry arch extending 75 feet into the tunnel from each portal, with the tunnel itself (without the arch) carved out to a height of 18 feet. This modest opening in the hillside was narrow—only 20 feet from wall to wall (though wider than the canal's 17-foot-wide locks)—and boats most likely were poled through its length.

Designed to arouse curiosity, the tunnel worked admirably as a promotional gimmick. People traveled miles to see it—many all the way up from Philadelphia—often making use of the canal in the process and discovering the existence of the new transportation route it provided. But the curiosity didn't last long and by the mid-1850s, the cover was simply removed, effectively replacing the historic tunnel with an open cut through the ridge.

Meanwhile, the Union Canal Company had been working on another part of the original Schuylkill and Susquehanna plan—or, that is, on a modification of it, connecting Reading with Middletown. With the threat of competition from New York's Erie Canal, Pennsylvania recognized the urgency of completing its own inland transportation connections. The state provided financial aid to the Union Canal Company, which completed its part of the link from the Susquehanna to Philadelphia between 1821 and 1828, a distance of 81 miles by canal.

The summit of the Union Canal, a little west of the town of Lebanon, became the site of the nation's second tunnel. For many years touted by the Lebanon County Historical Society as "the oldest [existing] tunnel in the United States," the Lebanon Tunnel (or Union Canal Tunnel) was carved out of slate rock mostly with picks and shovels aided by a little blasting. Begun in 1824, the last of its 729-foot length was completed in 1826. The total cost was $30,464. By

The Union Canal tunnel, second tunnel built in the United States. Courtesy of William Shank. Painting by Charles A. Bleistein

1828, boats began moving up and down the finished canal, propelled through the tunnel by poles, while the mules climbed over the watershed ridge to resume their towing job on the other side.

The hilly terrain of Pennsylvania also became the site of America's third tunnel, 850 feet long, driven on the Western Division Canal. The Western Division formed the western end of Pennsylvania's great east-west transportation system. The "Main Line," built between 1826 and 1834, connected Philadelphia, the state's eastern port on the Delaware River, with Pittsburgh, 300 miles to the west, at the junction of the Allegheny, Ohio and Monongahela rivers. The tunnel, completed in 1830, took the canal through a mountain ridge in the Allegheny Mountains, near Saltsburg and just east of Tunnelton, instead of following the Conemaugh River's meandering loop through lower terrain. The longest tunnel built in the United States at the time, it emerged on the other side directly onto an aqueduct that carried the canal across the Conemaugh River.

The Western Division Canal, which linked Pittsburgh to Johnstown on the Conemaugh, also boasted one other underground passage—the Grant's Hill Tunnel. Completed in August 1832, Grant's Hill was part of a compromise between old Pittsburgh, south of the Allegheny, and the newer community of Allegheny borough, on the north shore. Surveys had shown that the north shore approach for the Western Division Canal made better sense than coming along the south shore directly into Pittsburgh proper. But Pittsburgh merchants were outraged. So the north approach was used, but an extension was built, with an aqueduct across the river and a turning basin on the Pittsburgh side. This final phase of the canal trip on the "Main Line" was quaintly described by British author Charles Dickens, in his account of a trip he made to the United States in 1842:

On Monday evening furnace fires and clanking hammers on the banks of the canal warned us that we approached the termination of this part of our journey. After going through another dreamy place—a long aqueduct across the Allegheny River, . . . a vast, low, wooden chamber full of water—we emerged upon that ugly confusion of backs of buildings and crazy galleries and stairs which always abuts on water, whether it be river, sea, canal, or ditch; and were at Pittsburgh.

Today, this tunnel provides through access for highway traffic beneath a canal lock on the St. Lawrence Seaway. St. Lawrence Seaway Authority

Historical Headlines

1812–1830

1812   Americans declare war against Britain (War of 1812). The war lasts about two years.

Lewis Wernwag's "Colossus" bridge over the Schuylkill at Philadelphia is completed, with a span of 340 feet.

1816   World's first wire suspension bridge spans the Schuylkill River near Philadelphia.

1817   The western portion of Mississippi Territory becomes the 20th state, Mississippi.

Theodore Burr patents an "arch-and-truss" design for wooden bridges.

1820   Congress passes the Missouri Compromise, prohibiting slavery in the Louisiana Territory north of the Mason-Dixon Line, latitude 36°30′.

Ithiel Town obtains patent for the "Town Truss," a lattice-work design for building wooden bridges.

1824   America's first school of science and engineering opens, later called Rensselaer Polytechnic Institute.

1825   The Erie Canal is completed in New York State, connecting Buffalo, on Lake Erie, with Albany, on the Hudson River.

1827   The B&O Railroad is chartered by the State of Maryland (February 28). Construction begins July 4, 1828.

South Carolina grants permission to build the South Carolina Canal & Railroad, later part of the Southern Railroad (December 19).

1829   The "Stourbridge Lion," a locomotive imported from England, becomes the first steam locomotive to run on commercial track in the United States (August 8).

The world's oldest railroad bridge, the Carrollton Viaduct, is built by the B&O Railroad at Gwynn's Falls near Baltimore, Maryland.

1830   New York manufacturer Peter Cooper builds the "Tom Thumb," first commercially successful American steam locomotive. It loses race against a horse, however.

Stephen H. Long patents a design for iron and wood bridges.

First railroad timber bridge is built by Lewis Wernwag.

U.S. census counts 12.8 million people in the United States; 150,000 immigrants had arrived since 1820.

From this terminus, at the insistence of Pittsburgh downtowners, an additional arm of the canal was constructed, running through an 810-foot tunnel driven in Grant's Hill, to the south, and, via four locks, down to the Monongahela River. The Grant's Hill Tunnel extension came out on the river exactly where another canal, the Chesapeake and Ohio, was supposed to enter Pittsburgh. But that leg of the Chesa-

peake and Ohio was never built, and so the Grant's Hill tunnel never was used as much more than a drainpipe for spill water from the canal basin on the other side of the hill.

By now, in any case, a rival transportation force had appeared: the railroad. The first U.S. railroads—the Baltimore and Ohio Railroad and the South Carolina Canal and Railroad Company—were chartered in

1827, and by 1830 the B&O had begun its first daily runs. Although more canals were built after that, and canal tunnels as well, the days of the canals were numbered.

But with the railroad, whose locomotives could not climb the steep grades of the Allegheny and Appalachian Mountains, came a greater demand for tunnels. As a result, big advances would be made in the technology of tunnel building in the years that followed.

3

SAVING RAILWAY TIME: THE FIRST RAILROAD TUNNELS

Between 1830 and 1850, the railroads virtually transformed transportation in the United States. In 1830 only 23 miles of track had been laid. By 1840, just 10 years later, the number had increased to nearly 3,000 miles, and in the next 10 years doubled to more than 6,000 miles. As this enormous growth of the nation's rail system continued, builders faced the ever-increasing challenge of the rugged American terrain.

Early locomotives (and even later ones) didn't have the power to climb steep grades, and the best way to get to the other side of a mountain, therefore, was usually to cut a hole directly through it. If the summit was not too high above the railroad grade, this could be done, of course, by slicing an open cut just as the Schuylkill Navigation Company finally did on its tunnel. But deep cuts didn't work well. Dislodged by rain, soft earth and rocks would fall down the steep walls, blocking the track and often causing serious accidents. And in winter, snow would collect in the cuts in deep drifts that stopped traffic until they could be cleared away.

In 1831–32 the first railroad tunnel was driven by the Allegheny Portage Railroad in Pennsylvania. The tunnel formed part of the combination canal and railroad system known as the "Main Line of Improvement," which connected Philadelphia and Pittsburgh (the same "Main Line" that was com-

pleted at its western end by the Western Division Canal with its two canal tunnels).

In the beginning, Pennsylvanians conceived of the Main Line as one long canal, or a series of canals, running from east to west, straight through Allegheny Mountain, just south of Hollidaysburg. But the initial plan for getting a canal through Allegheny Mountain was never well thought through. The Main Line system was such a large project that the contractors, breaking ground in 1826, concentrated first on building the waterways on either side, which were almost complete by the time they began to think seriously about the mountain in 1828. As planned, the tunnel would pierce through 4 miles of rock-solid mountain—a virtually unthinkable feat when the only tunnels in the country were those built on the Schuylkill Navigation Canal, the Union Canal and the Western Division of the Main Line itself. The longest of these was only 850 feet. As canal and transportation historian William Shank writes, "Even today the digging of a four-mile tunnel would be a major undertaking. The prospect of such an enterprise in 1828 was overwhelming." In any case, the plan called for the canal to run through the tunnel so high up the mountain slope that it would still have required some fancy engineering to raise the water in the canal to the right level.

Realizing these obstacles, the commissioners came up with another idea: a portage railroad to take the canal freight and passengers over Allegheny Mountain between Hollidaysburg and Johnstown, on the Conemaugh River. Once on the other side, passengers and freight would transfer back to the canal. The idea was approved by the state legislature and signed into law by the governor in March 1831. But the portage railroad still needed a tunnel at the summit—a shorter tunnel, but a tunnel, nonetheless. So in 1831 the first railway tunnel in the United States was started.

The miners, who received $13 a month, carved out its 701-foot length using the "English system" of excavation—the same that later would be used on the Hoosac Tunnel. Tunneling engineers usually chose a system of excavation based on their own knowledge and experience as well as tunneling conditions, such as the type of rock and the possibility of dangerous cave-ins. The English system involved driving a pilot tunnel in the middle of what would later be the crown of the tunnel's arch. This pilot heading might measure about 10 feet wide and 18 feet high, actually about 3½ feet above what would eventually be the roof of the tunnel. Workers would brace the top of this pilot tunnel along the roof with two big timbers, called "crown bars," about 30 inches in diameter and 20 or 25 feet long. They propped these with vertical timbers extending to the floor of the tunnel. When the plans called for adding a masonry lining arch, as they did for the first 150 feet from each portal of the Allegheny Portage Tunnel, the workers would often prop one end of the "crown bars" on the finished masonry behind.

Once the pilot tunnel was excavated, the full width of the tunnel at the top would be dug out, two more crown bars would be added, and a horizontal sill across the width of the tunnel would provide a permanent brace. Props radiating from the crown to the sill distributed weight to the sides of the tunnel. The 20-foot section of tunnel was then hollowed out to its ultimate diameter through a complex system alternating digging and propping until the entire bore was complete, supported by props along the sides and often reinforced with a wooden lining or "lagging" against shifting earth or runs. In masonry-lined tunnels, the bricklayers would then begin work in the excavated section while the miners moved on to break out the pilot heading for the next section of tunnel, moving the crown bars forward as they carved out the face.

The total cost of the Allegheny Portage Railroad Tunnel project came to $37,798 or $1.47 for each cubic yard of excavation. Completed in 1833, it was 19 feet high and 20 feet wide, accommodating the Portage Railroad's double tracks. An arch of cut stone extended from each end a distance of 150 feet to provide additional bracing at the portals—as well as a more finished look at the tunnel entrances.

The Allegheny Portage Railroad opened for traffic in 1834, ascending to the summit at Blair's Gap with the help of five inclined planes. Another series of four inclined planes made the descent to Johnstown on the Conemaugh River on the western side of the slope. (An inclined plane was a kind of cable-assisted railway device that made up for inadequate horse power on a steep grade. Stationary steam engines at the top of a rise pulled wire or rope cables. On the double-tracked Allegheny Railroad, the weight of an ascending train was balanced by a descending train on the other side.) In the beginning, horses pulled the cars the distance between inclined planes on the Allegheny, but they were later replaced by steam locomotives. As a traveler making the trip in August 1835 remarked in his description of his journey:

> In six hours the cars and passengers were to be raised 1,172 feet of perpendicular height and be lowered 1,400 feet of perpendicular descent by complicated, powerful and frangible machinery, and were to pass a mountain, to overcome which with a similar weight three years ago would have required the space of three days.

In the end, the Main Line system also included a railroad from Philadelphia to Columbia, on the Susquehanna River, with an inclined plane at each end. By 1838, the canal began using sectional boats that could be loaded in wheeled cradles, making it possible for travelers to remain aboard their boats all the way from Philadelphia to Pittsburgh.

The second railway tunnel in the United States was the Black Rock Tunnel, built between 1835 and 1837 on the Philadelphia and Reading Railroad near Phoenixville, Pennsylvania. Originally a local coal road, the Philadelphia and Reading provided rail connections from the coal fields near the Schuylkill River around Reading to the market and port at Philadelphia. In the Black Rock Tunnel, for the first time, American tunnelers sank shafts (dug vertical access tunnels, a technique that had been used by

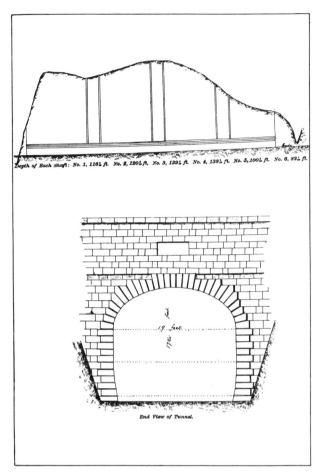

Depth of Each Shaft: No. 1, 116½ ft. No. 2, 120½ ft. No. 3, 139½ ft. No. 4, 133½ ft. No. 5, 100½ ft. No. 6, 82½ ft.

End View of Tunnel.

This profile of the Black Rock Tunnel, on the Philadelphia and Reading Railroad, shows how vertical shafts were dug to the depth of the main tunnel. These shafts provided ventilation and, in many cases, a way to remove excavated rock and dirt. Often, as in the Summit Tunnel on the Central Pacific, workers descended these shafts and worked from these additional faces to speed completion of the tunnel. J. L. Ringwalt, *The Development of Transportation Systems in the United States,* reprinted by permission of Johnson Reprint Corporation

ancient tunnelers), advancing the tunnel from the shafts by working in both directions from the new faces created in this way. The shafts not only increased the rate of work but also provided ventilation inside the tunnel. In all, workers sank a total of six shafts, ranging from a little over 82 feet to 139.4 feet deep, from the topside of the mountain.

The Black Rock Tunnel required excavation of 27,713 yards of rock from inside the tunnel, as well as removal of another 22,126 yards of rock at the ends. Inside the tunnel, workers also encountered a vein of soft earth that had to be timbered to keep it from caving in.

Since they were tunneling near an adjacent rival canal, the builders of the Black Rock faced yet another problem—cleaning up the material thrown onto the towpath. This part of the operation proved one of the greatest secondary expenses of the project. In addition, the Philadelphia and Reading had to remove stones thrown by workers and blasting into the canal itself, as well as reimburse a nearby factory for damage caused by blasting.

In all, the total costs for the 1,932-foot tunnel came in at $178,992. It was the largest and probably the most expensive tunnel built in the United States during the 1830s. By 1841 the Philadelphia and Reading had built two more tunnels in the coal fields, the Flat Rock Tunnel at Manayunk and the Pulpit Rock Tunnel at Port Clinton.

Even though the Philadelphia and Reading was first to build a railroad tunnel, the Baltimore and Ohio was close behind. Intent on extending its line from Baltimore, Maryland, to Wheeling, in what is now West Virginia, the B&O Railroad became one of the foremost early tunnel builders. By connecting the busy port of Baltimore with Wheeling on the Ohio River, a profitable flow of traffic could be established between the busy inland river trade—supported by the swelling number of Midwestern farmers and both markets and suppliers on the Atlantic Coast. But difficult mountain ranges had long blocked passage in this direction. The answer, the B&O saw, was tunnels. The Doe Gully Tunnel, a 1,207-foot bore built in 1839-41 by the B&O about 60 miles west of Harper's Ferry, was the longest U.S. tunnel completed before 1850. It cut through a mountain to avoid a snaking bend of the Potomac River, and its total cost came in at $98,426. Before the end of the decade, the B&O built four more tunnels at various locations, including one in 1839–40 that was 86 feet long at Harpers Ferry. Overall, the B&O drove 11 tunnels between Cumberland, Maryland and Wheeling alone.

Most of these tunnels, as well as most of the rest of the railroad tunnels built during this period, used what became known as the "American" system of tunneling. Compared to some of the complex European systems, which involved complicated sequences of excavation and intricate timbering, the American system was simple and straightforward. Except in very difficult ground, the tunnel was usually dug full face—the full bore all at once, without using a pilot tunnel as the English system did and without temporary trenches and so on. The roof was supported by a simple cap, made of a horizontal timber across the width of the tunnel braced by two sloping timbers. These braces rested in a notch cut in the rock at the top of the tunnel's vertical wall. Spaces between timbers were filled in by lumber lagging. Usually, this timber bracing was intended to be temporary, until the railroads could begin to make a profit. In some cases, as we'll see, this approach backfired. But the full-face method of tunneling has proved to be the method most commonly adopted for today's modern tunnels. In fact, the more complex European systems are no longer used.

Delays in building the early railway tunnels occurred frequently—but an incomplete tunnel usually meant an incomplete line, with disastrous effects on the railroad's profits and on the area's transportation links. Steep temporary bypass tracks called shooflies were often built, zigzagging over a mountain, until the tunnel could be driven through. The B&O's 4,100-foot Kingwood tunnel through the Laurel Mountains in what is now West Virginia, for example, was begun in 1849 but not finished until well into the 1860s. On the east side of the Kingwood tunnel, the B&O laid a steep, winding track over the top of the hill, rising 528 feet in a mile. To get supplies to the track layers on the other side of the mountain, a 25-ton coal-burning locomotive would puff up the mountain at 10–12 mph carrying a 15-ton load of rails. It was a feat easily enough accomplished on a clear, dry day—but on a wet track the wheels often locked on the locomotive, tender and cargo car, and the entire train slid all the way back down to the bottom of the hill.

The B&O had a similar problem with the Broad Tree Tunnel, where the railroad built a temporary road over the top of the ridge in 1852. This road was so steep that the zigzags included switches. Trains moved forward into a switch, then backed up onto the next section of track, continuing up the mountain to the next switch in reverse. But the road came in handy, not only during the completion of the tunnel, but also later, after traffic through the tunnel had already begun.

Originally, the Broad Tree's engineers thought the natural arch of rock in the tunnel would hold with just some timber bracing, such as the B&O had used in the Kingwood Tunnel. The single-track tunnel was only 16 feet wide and 22 feet high, and at first all seemed fine. But then the seams in the crumbly slate rock of the mountain began to give way, and the

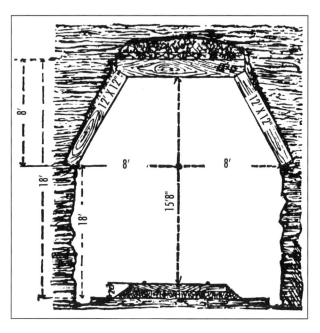

The American system of tunneling called for digging a tunnel full face and then supporting the roof with a timber cap. Courtesy of Holt, Rinehart and Winston

weight of rock settling against the timbers created such a strain that officials feared that the tunnel might collapse. So they decided to line the tunnel with stone walls and an arched roof of brick. The work, done in 1856 and 1857, was completed while the railroad continued its service as usual along the line.

The Broad Tree tunnel rock proved so treacherous that the project was haunted by accidents. Often, to remove the rock pressing down on the timber supports, workers had to blast the rock slabs, which then would come tumbling down, frequently destroying the timber supports in the process. As a result of these cave-ins and blockages, the tunnel was often unusable by the trains, which instead had to inch up over the steep shoofly track—luckily left in place after completion of the tunnel. In one instance, as the men inside the tunnel were working, a slab of rock fell suddenly from the ceiling, crushing five workers at once against the tunnel floor. Many others were killed or injured before the job was done.

The Broad Tree Tunnel experience was typical of many of the early B&O tunnels. In a rush to complete the line, the B&O had not lined most of its tunnels—and then had to add masonry or brick arched ceilings from two to six years later, when the rock began to give way and create dangerous conditions. By this time the traffic along the line had increased greatly, and

The Steam Drill

As far back as the Romans who used cold water to split scorched rock, tunnelers have always looked for ways to mechanize the slow, back-breaking tasks of drilling, digging and hammering. And between 1813 and 1850 in both Europe and the United States, several inventors came up with methods that worked. But it was a man named J. J. Couch of Philadelphia who invented the first steam-operated percussion rock drill, patented in 1849. This machine hurled a long, lancelike drill at the rock, then caught it as it bounced back, once again hurling it forward by making use of the forward action of the engine's piston. This relentless hammering process (or percussion drilling) chipped and broke the rock away with each hurling of the drill. The power for this drill was provided by a steam engine mounted on a dolly with wheels, and the drill itself was mounted on the housing of the steam engine.

A man working with Couch, Joseph Fowle, invented another, improved steam drill, which he patented in 1851. The Fowle drill, which became the granddaddy of all later rock drills, soon was operated using compressed air to power it instead of steam. Fowle, who did not have the money to develop his design further, sold his patent to Charles Burleigh in 1865. Burleigh developed some enhancements to the design, and the Burleigh compressed-air drill soon became famous for the job it did in the Hoosac Tunnel in Massachusetts. This evolution of the Burleigh drill from the earlier U.S. steam drill resulted in a design that made use of some of the older steam drill features, making it superior to any drills being used in the Alpine tunnels of Europe. And so, out of the American steam drill, was born a compressed-air-drill industry that would make history, not only in the Hoosac, but in the mines and tunnels of the American West and worldwide.

workers had to stop for frequently passing trains, wait for the smoke to clear, and then return to work. As a result, the cost of adding these linings later sometimes amounted to as much as six times as much as it would have cost the railroad to put them in at the time of construction. Some cost as much as $134 per running foot (for each foot of tunnel length) to arch. At the time of construction or immediately after, the B&O had arched, or lined, only two of its tunnels, the Doe Gully and the Paw Paw, which averaged a little over $22.50 a running foot for that part of the job. The average for adding arches to all the rest of the B&O tunnels between Baltimore and Wheeling was $77.31 a running foot. Although the profitable B&O line may not have been severely handicapped by these high costs, the lesson in tunneling was clear: Know the geology of the tunnel site and do it right the first time.

The third and fourth railway tunnels to be built in the United States were the Harlem Tunnel (1836–37) on the New York and Harlem Railroad (sometimes called the "Old" Harlem Tunnel) and the Elizabethtown (1835–38) between Harrisburg and Lancaster on part of what later became the Pennsylvania Rail-

road. The Harlem Tunnel measured 844 feet, while the Elizabethtown was 900 feet.

By 1850, 29 railway tunnels had been built in America. In contrast, tunnels built on canals by that time numbered only seven, none of them built after 1838. Railways were taking over as the nation's main transportation system, and more and more tunnels were needed. Overall, constructing these early railway tunnels was difficult, dangerous and expensive, with costs ranging from $500,000 to $1 million a mile. Although blasting powder was used, the holes for the powder were drilled by hand and the rest of the back-breaking work was done with picks and shovels.

By 1870, though, the times were changing, and people began to see that some of the work might be mechanized. In 1849, J. J. Couch of Philadelphia had invented the steam drill, touted as "the first promising labor-saving device for drilling rocks." J. W. Fowle, who had assisted him, developed an improved version that same year. (See box.) While strong, courageous men like the folk hero John Henry fought to keep pace, steam drills began to be introduced, and tunneling hovered on the verge of new breakthroughs. John

Human Strength vs. Steam Drill Might:
John Henry and the Big Bend Tunnel

John Henry had one of the lowest and worst paying jobs on the railroad: He was "a steel drivin' man." Swinging a heavy hammer, he drove holes into the solid rock for the explosives that would blast it away. John Henry's job wasn't one that many men envied but he was good at it, the best hammer-swinging man around, people said in those days, and he took great pride in his abilities at "drivin' steel."

The legend of John Henry began somewhere around 1870 during the building of the Big Bend Tunnel in West Virginia. Every town likes to claim a hero as its own, and the stories springing up around the country usually found Big John Henry working on whatever railroad tunnel happened to be the closest to the particular town where the story was being told. Some diligent detective work by folklore specialists, though, has pretty much established the Big Bend Tunnel in West Virginia as the place, and a 6-foot-tall, 200-pound black steel driver from North Carolina as being the most likely "true" John Henry.

As the story is usually told, John Henry was the biggest and strongest man on the work crew, able to outperform any three men in hammering the holes into the rocks that would later be used by the railroad's dynamite men. He was a quiet, modest man away from the job, a big man, they said, who "wouldn't hurt a flea." But on the job, swinging his hammer, he was a proud man, given to singing snatches of song to keep the work crew's rhythm in step to his own driving pace. John Henry was liked and respected by all. Respect was the balm that soothed the hard work of the steel-driving crews, and John Henry was a man who held his head up high, even while swinging his 12-pound hammer in the blistering heat and dust of the long, hot work days.

But times were changing. Just as the powerful locomotives were replacing the slower horse-drawn wagons, a new invention called the steam drill was being used by some of the railroad crews to do John Henry's job. In fact, in one version of the story, the crew working the other side of the tunnel from John Henry's crew was already using the new drill to bore its dynamite holes. What is known for certain is that one day, one way or another, one of the new steam drills showed up where John Henry and his steel-driving crew mates were working. What happened next usually depends upon who is telling the story.

In some versions John Henry's own crew boss, his "captain," challenges John Henry to try and beat the job done by the powerful steam driven machine. In other versions "the Captain," proud of his crew, makes a bet with an opposing crew boss that his best man, John Henry, can outperform the fancy new machine.

A contest was quickly arranged. Picking up two heavy, 20-pound hammers, one for each hand, John Henry took up his stance next to the man operating the powerful new steam drill. At the signal, man and machine began their arduous duel. For 35 long minutes the battle raged. The steam drill hissed and screamed as it cut deep, and John Henry's muscles strained and ached as he swung first one hammer and then the other against the two steel "spikes" that punched two separate holes into the rock. By the time it was over John Henry had dug two holes, each 7 feet deep, and the steam drill had completed only one 9-foot hole. Amidst the cheers and congratulations of the excited men, John Henry quietly collected his share of the bets that had been placed and holding his head up high returned to his home and his wife, Polly Ann.

That night, according to the legend, John Henry died when a blood vessel burst inside his head, brought on, people said, by his heroic battle against the steam drill.

Whether the real John Henry died that night or not is a matter of some dispute. Some researchers believe that he lived and simply moved on to another job after the Big Bend tunnel was completed. Still others maintain that he was killed months later in an explosion before the Big Bend was finished.

But whether John Henry lived or died after his heroic battle against the steam drill, his story lives on today in both legend and song.

Historical Headlines

1831–1850

1832	First streetcar (horsedrawn) in the world begins operating in New York City (New York and Harlem Railroad).
1834	Cyrus McCormick of Virginia patents first successful mechanical reaper.
1836	Texas becomes a republic independent from Mexico; Samuel Houston is president.
	Wernwag builds bridge for B&O Railroad at Harpers Ferry, crossing the Potomac into Philadelphia.
1836–39	First iron-arch bridge in the United States, at Brownsville, Pennsylvania, designed by Richard Delafield. It survived without change up to 1921.
1840	Sixth national census shows U.S. population has swelled to 17 million.
	Three thousand miles of railroad track already have begun to connect parts of the nation.
	Trouble with railroad bridges begins: A wooden Town Truss railroad bridge over Catskill Creek in New York collapses, causing the first U.S. fatality in such an accident.
	William Howe patents a new, stronger truss design, incorporating the use of iron rods.
1844	Thomas Pratt and his father Caleb patent a bridge design combining iron and wood.
1845	First iron-truss bridge built in the United States, by the Philadelphia and Reading Railroad, spans a creek in Pennsylvania on the Delaware River's west bank opposite Manayunk (which is now part of Philadelphia).
1846	Baltimore and Susquehanna Railroad builds an iron girder bridge at Bolton Station, Maryland, 1846–47.
1848	Gold discovered at John Sutter's camp in California, setting off the gold rush of 1849 the following year.
	The Starrucca Viaduct, the first U.S. bridge with concrete piers, is built near Susquehanna, Pennsylvania, to span a deep valley as the New York and Erie Railroad pushed toward Binghamton, New York. It is now a national landmark.
1849	Pacific Railroad Company, first railroad west of the Mississippi, is chartered.
1850	Overland mail delivery is established for the first time west of the Missouri River, from Independence, Missouri to Ogden, Utah.

Henry's legendary words still echo in the folksong, ". . . before I let that steam drill get me down, I'll die with a hammer in my hand, Lawd, Lawd, I'll die with a hammer in my hand." But while the legend of John Henry still lives on today, the age of mechanized tunneling had come to America, and a rocky mountain in western Massachusetts would turn out to be the proving ground for some of 19th-century tunneling's biggest breakthroughs. That progress, however, was destined to start out very slowly.

4

"THE BIG BORE": TUNNELING THROUGH THE HOOSAC 1855–76

Originally, the plan for a tunnel through the Hoosac Mountain in western Massachusetts developed around 1820 in the minds of nervous Bostonians. They clearly foresaw that the Erie Canal, begun between New York and Buffalo in 1817, was going to pull trade away from Boston Harbor. So they thought they could cut in on some of that traffic by building a canal that would connect Boston with the Hudson River—through the Hoosac Mountain. However, by 1830, railroads began to appear on the American transportation scene, and by 1848 canal building no longer seemed like a worthwhile investment. Railroads could operate year-round, while canals froze over during the cold New England winters. Railroads were easier and cheaper to build, especially over rough, hilly terrain. And railroad trains, even the early models traveling at speeds of 10 or 12 mph, got there faster than the canal boats that floated along at an average of only 6 mph.

And so the idea of a railroad tunnel through the Hoosac was born. A company known as the Troy and Greenfield Railroad was formed, having filed a petition for a charter in 1848 with the State of Massachusetts. The Troy and Greenfield planned to use roughly the same route that had originally been planned for the canal—completing the link between eastern lines in Greenfield (in western Massachusetts), through

the Deerfield and Hoosac valleys to the state line, to another railway line that would close the connection to Troy, New York, on the Hudson. By 1854, the Troy and Greenfield had persuaded the Massachusetts State Legislature to pass an act "to enable the Company to construct the Hoosac Tunnel." The railroad also received a commitment from the state for $2 million toward construction of the tunnel, an action that opened up a Pandora's box of troubles for Massachusetts state legislators, who set up a commission to oversee the tunnel's construction.

While the Hoosac Tunnel was not the first railroad tunnel in the United States, nor, certainly the last, it has become the most famous. Building it took over 21 years and probably more than $10 million (though estimates vary)—nearly exhausting the treasury of the State of Massachusetts. The project went through five contractors, four site engineers and a number of commissioners. In one year alone, workers dulled 153,436 drill bits and exploded 11,195 pounds of powder to remove only 2,329 cubic yards of mountain. At the time work on the tunnel began, none of the great tunnels that soon would be driven through the rocky Alps in Switzerland had yet been built. The planned Hoosac Tunnel was long— 4¾ miles—and the Hoosac Mountain was made of solid rock—hard

The mouth of the Hoosac Tunnel during construction. Smithsonian Institution   PHOTO NO. 16524

gneiss, micaschist and granitic gneiss. But, overall, as a tunneling job, it was not that difficult. Yet, political haggling and miscalculations made the work so slow that punsters throughout the state soon called it "The Big Bore," and most people began to think they would not see it completed within their lifetimes. As poet Oliver Wendell Holmes put it dryly, "When the first locomotive rolls through the Hoosac Tunnel bore, then order your ascension robes."

But the Hoosac would mark a key turning point in the history of tunneling in America. In 1855, when work began on the tunnel in earnest, most tunnel excavation was still done with hand equipment—picks, shovels, hammers, wedges and manual drills. By its completion, a new industry had been born in the

United States—the compressed-air industry—putting U.S. manufacturers at the world forefront in the development of the first mechanized tools for digging underground. The Hoosac Tunnel was also one of the first projects to use nitroglycerin, as well as steam drills.

The Hoosac's problems began, though, at the outset, with the original estimates for the tunnel's costs. Planners severely underestimated the cost at $1,948,557, setting up everyone concerned for disappointment from the beginning. Estimator A. F. Edwards predicted that the project would take just 1,556 days, which turned out to be less than a fifth of the time that it actually took to complete the tunnel. It was further estimated that if a central shaft were used, the work would go even faster, taking only 1,054 days.

That could be trimmed even further to 1,005 days, Edwards maintained, by using a giant steam-powered machine in the excavation.

The Wilson machine, as it was called, weighed 70 tons, with several drills mounted to drill a circular groove 13 inches wide and 24 feet in diameter around the circumference of the tunnel. The core inside this circle was then blasted out. By 1853 it had already been set to work experimentally at the Hoosac but completed only about 10 feet of excavation before money for the experiment ran out. Even if that had not happened, though, it's not clear what plan the engineers envisioned for getting steam power to the big drilling machine as it moved deeper into the tunnel. The Wilson Machine was replaced by another, called the Talbot Tunneling Machine, which was designed to cut a core 17 feet across. A third machine, from New York, designed to cut a core 8 feet in diameter, was also tried out.

These giant machines accomplished very little, though, and the State of Massachusetts was left disappointed. B. H. Latrobe, who later became a consulting engineer on the Hoosac and built many tunnels for the B&O Railroad, testified before the committee in 1862: "The novel and ingenious machines for driving the tunnel, either by annular groove or a cylinder bore in the center of the section I could entertain no confidence in, as they require the machines to do too much of the work and the powder too little." The machine's inventors, evidently, were trying to push the results of technology too fast, but as we know today, their visions were not so far off as Latrobe seemed to think.

No financial investors were found who were willing to tackle this giant, long-term project. In fact, if potential backers had been able to foresee the future, they would have been even less enthusiastic. But a series of hopeful contractors did take a crack at it partly on speculation. The first, E. W. Serrel & Co., began work in 1855. They completed little work, though, and quit within a year. The second, Herman Haupt & Co., entered the picture in 1858. In exchange for building a railway and tunnel as well as raising the money for it, Haupt & Co. asked for nearly $3 million in bonds and another $1.1 million in cash. They got the go-ahead from the legislature and set to work. But progress ended in June 1861 when the state reneged on a payment. Amid charges of corruption and misdealing, Haupt & Co. resigned, and so ended the second contract. With the Civil War raging, the U.S. government was only too glad to set Haupt & Co. to work repairing bridges damaged by Confederate troops. Before the war was over, Herman Haupt and his crews, along with those in charge of the military railroads, had repaired 26 miles of bridges, rebuilding some of them in as little as two weeks. Haupt & Co. was finally vindicated many years later in the Hoosac matter, when the Massachusetts State Legislature awarded payments to the company in 1884.

At the time, though, the outrage over the Hoosac seemed justified, if, as it turned out, misplaced. In six years, progress on the tunnel amounted to a 306-foot shaft and a 1,850-foot tunnel advancing westward from the shaft, plus another section of the tunnel extending 2,400 feet westward from the east portal.

No further work progressed on the tunnel until 1863. At this point, with 20,166 feet of tunnel remaining to be driven, the State of Massachusetts took charge. Recognizing that a new approach needed to be taken to the insurmountable Hoosac, the state sent an engineer to Europe. There tunnelers were making use of new methods to carve out the long Mont Cenis Tunnel beneath the Alps between France and Italy. And they had begun to use a compressed-air drill invented by Germain Sommeiller in 1861 that doubled the drilling rate. In the meantime, the excavation beneath the Hoosac Mountain made little progress, except for work on one oval shaft. However, work crews spent the time damming the Deerfield River to obtain power for the new compressors that the state commission planned to install.

By 1865, with the Deerfield dammed, workers began digging in earnest, this time using a "top heading" instead of a "bottom heading." That is, instead of excavating from the bottom up, they ran their pilot tunnel (using the English system) along the crown of the arch. They worked on three faces, with each heading 15 feet wide and 6 feet high, at an excruciatingly slow rate. By the end of the year, 9,522 man-days had been spent to gain a total of only 634 feet. The work was not going well. It took the equivalent of one man working more than three and a half days to remove just one cubic yard of the stubborn rock. The cost per yard of excavation continued to grow as call after call was made on state treasury funds. Irate Massachusetts citizens began to level accusations that the funds had been diverted to line the pockets of officials.

In the meantime, the engineers, impressed by what they had seen at Mont Cenis, thought they had a solution. Although Sommeiller had refused to let the American tunnelers use his design, both the commission and resident engineer Thomas Doane were convinced of compressed air's superiority over steam. To power the steam drills then being used in the Hoosac, steam had to be piped to the tunnel face from a boiler at the mouth of the tunnel. As the crews penetrated farther into the mountain, more and more power was lost. In addition, the hot, stuffy atmosphere deep inside the tunnel where the crews worked was only made worse by the steam and the exhaust from the drills. The use of compressed air would solve all of these problems. So, the Hoosac engineers set about designing their own compressed-air drill, and on October 31, 1866, the tunnel commission made a historic move, setting Burleigh rock drills to work in the east heading of the Hoosac. Designed by Charles Burleigh of Fitchburg, Massachusetts, their power was supplied by a mechanical compressor invented by Doane.

Oddly enough, though, the introduction of machine drilling did not seem to increase the speed right away. The new technology just cost more. Using manual methods and gunpowder, excavation of a cubic yard of rock took 3.6 man-days in 1865. Perhaps the going was tougher (veins of hard quartz in the mountain were referred to by one engineer as "unyielding as iron"). But the following year, with the Burleigh drills, excavating a cubic yard of rock actually took longer—4.3 man-days—and used 6.7 pounds of powder.

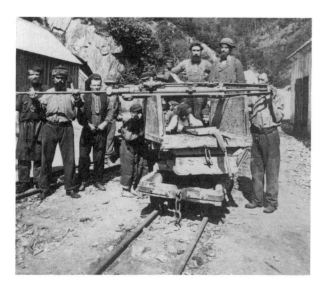

Workers with the tunnel rock drill used in the Hoosac. Smithsonian Institution PHOTO NO. 81-5767

That same year Doane also introduced electrical firing—the use of an electric spark to set off an explosion of powder. And Doane began experimenting with nitroglycerin, brought in from Europe. He invited chemist George M. Mowbray, who had used nitro successfully in the oil fields of Pennsylvania, to consult. Doane saw several advantages in using nitro. It was much more powerful than conventional powder. Deeper holes could be used for nitro, and therefore larger chunks of rock could be blasted loose. And it did not give off the noxious fumes that plagued workers using powder.

But, while nitroglycerin and electric firing eventually sped the progress, they also introduced extreme hazards to the work force. Nitro was notorious for its instability—especially before its discoverer, Alfred Nobel, found a way to stabilize it in 1868. Accidental detonations in the Hoosac occurred frequently and with deadly results. And the electrical firing, while efficient, also presented safety hazards. One man, walking through the tunnel in rubber boots that insulated him, unknowingly became a sort of human battery. So when he picked up a bare wire connection to a charge of explosives, the worker and everything around him were blown to bits. Estimates place the cost in lives for construction of the Hoosac Tunnel, from start to finish, at 196.

Finally frustrated, Thomas Doane resigned in 1867. But he had laid the groundwork for the technological advances that would make the Hoosac Tunnel famous in American tunneling.

After Doane left, another chief engineer took over briefly. Then the State Commission hired a contractor to proceed with the work and tried running the show without a chief engineer, each member of the Commission taking a turn being in charge. Three months later, when the contractor failed to work out, the Commission hired a fourth contractor to drive the tunnel eastward from the west portal. Then a fire, started by exploding lamp oil, broke out in the timber bracing of the central shaft. Thirteen men working at the bottom of the shaft were trapped as the flames roared up the flue created by the opening. All 13 men died, either burned or suffocated to death. The contractor resigned. Work on the shaft stopped for a year, the hole full of water, with the bodies of the dead workers trapped beneath.

By 1867, the experiment of driving the tunnel under direct Commission supervision had been less than successful, costing more than three times as

Work crews at the portal of the Hoosac. Notice the crane carrying rock. Smithsonian Institution   PHOTO NO. 90-16526

much per cubic yard of progress ($24.46) as the project had under the last contractor before the commissioners took over ($7.25).

In 1868, though, two new headings were opened up when a shaft started by Doane was completed. From this 318-foot shaft, located 3,000 feet east of the western portal of the tunnel, crews began working in both directions. This western shaft was supplied, and blasted materials were removed, by means of a big, steam-driven elevator. By June, on another heading at the west end of the tunnel, a drill carriage was introduced that could hold five drills all at one time. And

by August Mowbray started up a nitro factory in North Adams, a little village near the west portal of the tunnel. A posted sign warned: "Nitro-Glycerine Works. Dangerous! No Visitors Admitted."

On December 24, 1868, a new contractor entered the scene, the Shanly Brothers of Montreal, with a commitment to complete the job by March 1, 1874. Short of cash for the half-million dollars' deposit required for the deal, the Shanlys agreed to accept payment for the first half-million dollars' worth of work after completion of the tunnel. Two-thirds of the total distance of the tunnel still remained to be driven,

Electric Explosive Firing, Nitroglycerin and Dynamite

Powder was used for blasting from the first day of the excavation in 1855 of the Hoosac Mountain. At the working face of the tunnel, holes were drilled by men swinging 10-pound sheep-nosed hammers or by various machines. These holes were packed with powder, then plugged. A groove in each plug allowed insertion of a match or fuse, which then was lit. When ignited, the powder released gases with explosive force, and chunks of rock flew in every direction.

Electric firing was introduced in the Hoosac Tunnel by resident engineer Thomas Doane by 1866, greatly improving the safety of setting off a blast. But a worker could still set off an explosion by accidentally crossing two wires or just by holding one lead in his right hand and the other in his left, the electricity running through his body to complete the circuit. And to make matters worse the slowness of excavation on the Hoosac had already become a state-wide embarrassment. The engineers needed something that would cut more swiftly through the hard rock of the Hoosac Mountain.

In 1846, a chemist named Ascanio Sobrero at the Turin Institute of Technology in Italy discovered he could create a powerful liquid explosive by dripping glycerine slowly into strong sulfuric and nitric acids. The resulting oily yellow liquid, which he called nitroglycerin, could release 12,000 times the volume of gas it contained. However, no one knew how to set off a nitro explosion at will until 1859, when Alfred Nobel, a Swedish engineer, found a way. He discovered that nitro required a shock or, as he wrote in his patent, "an impulse of explosion," such as the one gunpowder might produce. Its one drawback was its great instability. On a scale that designates any rating below 100 as unstable and unsafe, nitro had a sensitivity rating of 13.

By 1866, though, Doane recognized the usefulness of this newfangled explosive for blasting through the hard rock of the Hoosac. Simultaneously, engineers at the Mont Cenis Tunnel in the Alps had begun to use nitro, too, and so did James Strobridge, tunneling for the Central Pacific Railroad in the High Sierra in California. Because only small holes were needed for nitro, drilling time could be cut. And this high explosive's tremendous power could easily shatter the steely rock of mountains like the Hoosac and the Sierra Nevada chain.

Cool temperatures could calm the unstable nature of the explosive liquid, but by 1867 Nobel had patented a new, more practical invention, dynamite. Dynamite was nitroglycerin made less sensitive to shock by adding another substance, such as a type of siliceous earth. A detonating cap was added to this much safer explosive so that it could be blown up at will—not by chance. Dynamite quickly replaced nitroglycerin at most construction sites, once it became known, although it still had some drawbacks, including deadly fumes and high expense.

and none of the tunnel so far completed was broken out to the two-track, 20-foot-high bore the contract called for. The Shanly crews would have to move faster than any crew had before.

By early 1869, work had begun again in earnest, with crews beginning to advance the east heading in March. Work on sinking the central shaft resumed in May and was completed by August of the following year. By July, progress began again on the west heading (though flooding caused by heavy rains would stop work here for several days in early October 1870). By December 1869, the Shanly Brothers had 700 men working at the Hoosac, and the new drilling machines finally began to pay off.

Improved machinery cut the cost of drilling by two-thirds, according to the contractor, with a total advance of 1,514 feet made in 1870. In 1866 manual drilling and gunpowder had yielded only 47.54 feet per month in progress as opposed to 126.17 feet per month in 1870. As workers became more experienced with the power drills, the speed of progress continued to increase, peaking in 1873 when 162 feet was excavated in one month. Workers tunneling toward each other on the two west headings met on November 27, 1873, and the two east headings met on December 12 of the same year. The surveying, it turned out, was the Hoosac Tunnel's best feature. At the points of breakthrough, the east headings were only 5/16 inch out of

Tunnelers—with their Burleigh drill—descending the west shaft of the Hoosac Tunnel for a day's work. Smithsonian Institution PHOTO NO. 88-18477

alignment, with only a few hundredths of a foot difference in grade, while the west headings were off only 9/16 inch, with a very small difference in level as well.

By December 22, 1874, the Shanly Brothers had completed their part of the contract, about nine months after their deadline, a small amount of time considering how late the overall project was running. But the tunnel lining still had to be done. Over the years of exposure, many areas of the rock had become eroded by water percolating through some of the veins, and some of the rock threatened to break loose. About 2,500 linear feet of the tunnel had to be lined, and completing that part of the project took until January 1, 1876. With the Hoosac finished at last, the official opening took place on July 1, 1876.

The cost, however, had been phenomenal. The Shanly Brothers received $4,594,268 for the portion of the tunnel they built. This phase alone cost more than twice as much as the original estimate for $1,948,557, and before the Shanly's began the state had already spent $3,002,176. As Ashbel Welch, a former president of the American Society of Civil Engineers, once said, "That is the best engineering,

The finished Hoosac portal, 1874. Smithsonian Institution   PHOTO NO. 90-16523

not which makes the most splendid, or even the most perfect, work, but that which makes a work that answers the purpose well, at the least cost." By this definition the Hoosac, clearly, was not an example of great engineering. Exact final figures as to its cost apparently do not exist, but one number mentioned in legislative records years later was $14,000,000. The Mont Cenis Tunnel through the Alps, which was nearly twice as long and took only 15 years to complete, cost little more—only $15,000,000.

The Hoosac Tunnel

Begun: 1855
Completed: 1876
Purpose: Railroad tunnel
Length: 4.75 miles
Width: 26 feet
Height: 21.5 feet

In the end, the Hoosac Tunnel never served its intended purpose: to provide Boston with a way to tap the western trade that was pouring into New York. Its greatest contribution, instead, was a technological legacy: giving birth to the compressed-air-drill industry in the United States. As civil engineer Thomas Curtis Clarke wrote in 1889, ". . . our labors are greatly assisted by the use of power-drills worked by compressed air and by the use of high explosives. . . . Rocks can now be removed in less than half the time formerly required, when ordinary blasting powder was used in hand-drilled holes."

Meanwhile, 3,000 miles away from the Hoosac, metal miners—seeking gold, silver and other ores in the craggy mountains of the Far West—benefited from these breakthroughs. And so did the progress of tunneling through those same mountains as the great railroads pierced the barriers between east and west.

5

ROCKY CONQUESTS: BUILDING RAILROAD TUNNELS IN THE FAR WEST

Along the western edge of North America, a series of spiny ridges runs from north to south—the Rocky Mountains (in many places dividing the flow of water to the east and west in what is known as the Continental Divide), the Cascade Mountains and the Sierra Nevada. All of them served as formidable blocks to the westward movement of America's railways, their rocky mountain passes too steep for early locomotives to climb, and the most impregnable of all was the great Sierra Nevada that blocked the east-west traffic to California. Yet people dreamed of a transcontinental railroad almost from the birth of rail transport in the United States. A writer for *The Emigrant*, a weekly newspaper published in Ann Arbor, Michigan, envisioned a railroad project connecting New York and Oregon as early as 1832.

In 1844, Asa Whitney of New York made another, more persuasive proposal. A transcontinental line, he said, would establish a rich trade link between the West Coast of the United States and ships crossing the Pacific from the Orient. But the undertaking remained blocked by political squabbles about routes and financing. So, in the 1840s, even as the network of railroads continued to grow east of the Mississippi, the great challenge of extending rails across the Great Plains and the Continental Divide, from coast to coast, still remained unmet.

Then with the discovery of gold in 1848 at Sutter's Mill in California, more and more people became eager to go west. But the available means of reaching the West Coast in those days were anything but efficient. To reach the West from the East Coast, travelers would first have to sail to Central America. From there they would cross the Isthmus of Panama by a succession of stagecoaches to the Pacific Ocean, where they could catch another ship to San Francisco, located to the north on the California coast. It was a long, arduous and spirit-numbing journey, but the options—sailing the long way around South America's Cape Horn, or making the entire voyage by slow wagon trains across the dangerous American prairie—weren't much more attractive.

Rail transportation to the Far West began to look profitable—and by 1853 Congress had set aside $150,000 and authorized a survey for a transcontinental railroad to the Pacific. Yet no plans took shape. Then a young engineer named Theodore Dehone Judah, newly arrived in California from Connecticut, took up the cause. He made the long trip east to try to stir up fresh interest in Washington in what he saw as the greatest transportation idea of the century. But by the late 1850s, during the prelude to the Civil War, the federal government had become focused on the more pressing issues of slavery and secession. And almost everyone, both in the East and in California, saw the rugged slopes of the Sierra Nevada range as an insurmountable obstacle. Far steeper than the Appalachians and the Alleghenies, the Sierra Nevada was unforgiving and treacherous—many hapless pioneers had already died trying to find their way across its summits. And no route usable to a railroad was known to exist. Judah found little interest and returned to California disappointed.

But by this time a few Californians had begun to see that a railroad link to the East could be of great value to their state's economy, and they held a Pacific Railroad Convention in 1859. The following year Judah set out to prove a key point—that he could survey a railroad route through the Sierra Nevada. He spent the summer exploring the rough mining country on the western slopes, looking for a way to cut through from the broad, flat valley of California's Sacramento River to the desert plains of Nevada. Donner Pass, where 47 pioneers had died trying to cross in the winter of 1864, became part of his route, along with Emigrant Pass and a mining road along the Truckee River. Ultimately, tunnels through the Sierra Nevada's hard granite would play an important part in the plan. That fall, with the help of Daniel Strong, a druggist in the mining town of Dutch Flat, Judah mapped out the route and a proposal, and in June 1861, in a small room over a Sacramento hardware store, Judah persuaded four wealthy merchants—Leland Stanford, Charles Crocker, Collis P. Huntington and Mark Hopkins—to finance his proposed "Central Pacific Railroad."

Soon known as "The Big Four," Judah's backers immediately sent him east on a second trip to lobby for government support, and this time the moment was right. The Civil War had broken out between the Northern and Southern States in 1861. Recently elected president, Abraham Lincoln recognized the importance of keeping California and its wealth solidly in the Union and willingly signed the Pacific Railroad Act into law in 1862. The act decreed that two lines, with considerable government assistance, would connect to create the nation's first transcontinental railroad.

The Central Pacific would extend eastward from Sacramento, while another railroad, the newly formed Union Pacific, would start at the Missouri River in Nebraska and extend westward toward Utah. Each railroad, eager for as large a share as possible in the potential profits, raced to lay the most track before the two lines finally met. In fact, by the time Judah returned to Sacramento, his four backers had already begun to "move mountains." Having persuaded a geologist to declare that the foothills of the Sierra Nevada actually started just outside of Sacramento (when in fact they are at least 31 miles away), the Central Pacific began laying track. Since the U.S. government subsidized $12,000 a mile on level ground and four times as much—$48,000 a mile—for laying track over the more difficult mountain terrain, the Big Four began collecting a tidy sum early in the game. Judah, who objected to such dishonesty, was unceremoniously forced out.

THE CENTRAL PACIFIC'S CHALLENGE: THE SIERRA NEVADA

Using a silver spade, Governor Leland Stanford broke ground in Sacramento on January 8, 1863. Of course, supplies from East Coast factories—including rails, spikes, tools and rolling stock—had to pass through Central America or come around the Horn by ship. But eventually they began to arrive, and the Central Pacific began to build. Most of the ground covered in the beginning was relatively flat, but the rugged mountains of the Sierra range loomed ahead, and, as it moved up into the foothills, the railroad developed acute labor problems.

The work was hard and wages were low. For many, prospecting for gold seemed more rewarding than toiling on a railroad—collecting 75 cents a day to fight dirt, mountains, brutal line bosses and freezing snow. To solve the railroad's labor shortage, Charles Crocker thought of hiring some of the many Chinese immigrants who had come to California in the early days of the gold rush. Although some had struck it rich and returned home, many others had stayed on to work as laborers, farmers, house servants for the wealthy, and workers in restaurants, laundries and other city jobs. Crocker offered jobs on the railroad to only a handful at first. The Chinese workers proved to be industrious, inventive and hard-working. Pleased with their performance, Crocker decided to hire more. In fact, after signing up all the Chinese workers he could in California, according to some sources, he sent agents to China to recruit even more. By the summer of 1866 more than 6,000 Chinese workers were laboring on the Central Pacific rails.

A Chinese worker, probably on his way back from carrying tea to fellow workers in the Central Pacific tunnel in the background. The Chinese workers' custom of drinking tea (for which water had to be boiled) probably contributed to their comparative good health during their work for the railroad. Association of American Railroads

Before construction was finished Crocker would employ over 12,000 on the line.

The Chinese crews began to push the Central Pacific roadbed eastward through the mountains. As one diarist described the scene in his journal in 1865, "They are laying siege to Nature in her strongest citadel . . . the rugged mountains . . . swarm with [laborers], shoveling, wheeling, carting, drilling and blasting rocks and earth . . ." By the end of November 1866, the Central Pacific reached Cisco, a five-hour rail trip over the newly laid tracks from Sacramento. The line covered 94 miles.

But as the tracks approached the summit, progress stopped dead while workers began to struggle with their greatest challenge, the dangerous task of punching a series of tunnels through the unyielding Sierra

granite. The difficulty of the problem was no secret. Early in the race with the Union Pacific, the UP had sent a representative to evaluate the competition. The 1,659-foot Summit Tunnel alone, he concluded, would take three years to complete.

But if the Central Pacific was to make a good share of the profit, the western railroad could not take three years. Work on the approach cuts to the Summit Tunnel began in 1865, and during the following year crews worked on all the approaches around the clock in three eight-hour shifts. To hurry the work on the Summit Tunnel, locomotives, cars and rails had been transported over the summit, to the Truckee Valley on the eastern slope. There digging began, while at the same time workers began tunneling through from the west. A third opening, a vertical shaft from the summit, was completed in December 1866, enabling work to proceed in both directions from the middle, as well. Inside, small crews of men chipped at the four faces in the lonely cold, while hundreds of others scratched at six other tunnels on the Sierra face, a total of seven tunnels in one 2-mile stretch.

Compared to the tunnels of the East, the CP tunnels were narrow—16 feet wide at the bottom and 11 feet high, topped with an arched ceiling having a 16-foot diameter. Most of them, carved out of solid granite, did not need to be lined, except for Tunnel 11, which was partly lined, and Tunnel 13, which required a complete lining of timber. These tunnels, driven through mixed soil instead of solid granite, were excavated slightly larger to allow for later addition of the masonry lining. Soon after the CP railroad line opened, however, all the tunnel sections had to be increased in size, so that the larger locomotives and cars that soon became commonplace could make it through the tunnel bores.

Overall, the tunnel work progressed extremely slowly. Often the Chinese workers could chisel and pick away no more than 8 inches a day from the granite face of the Sierra.

Nature now challenged the railroaders, not only with the formidable mountains, but with one of the worst winters the state had seen in many years. The snow began to fall in October 1866. Hard-packed snow in one valley measured 18 feet, with a total snowfall for the season of more than 44 feet. Storm after storm swept in across the Pacific Ocean to break against the Sierra peaks. By the time the tracks had reached a 6,000-foot elevation, each day's work had become an exercise in survival.

Through the heavily crusted snow, Chinese laborers burrowed a labyrinth of surface tunnels from their half-buried shacks to the mouth of the railroad tunnel, dug air shafts and chimney holes, chiseled stairways of ice and used lanterns for light.

Blizzards raged and avalanches were a constant danger. In one of the winter's worst accidents an entire camp—men, tents, buildings and machines—was swept away to be buried under the snow at the bottom of a canyon. There were no survivors, and the bodies, impossible to recover, had to lay frozen and buried under the snow until spring. Smaller avalanches took other workers, one, two or three at a time.

While pick-axes and shovels served well for building a railroad through the lowlands, the rocky slopes of the Sierra Nevada posed a less easily penetrable obstacle. Tons of black powder were imported from the East—powder manufactured in the West was inferior and only the best had any chance against Sierra granite. But even the best was not powerful enough.

By the winter of 1866–67, frustrated by the slow progress, superintendent of construction James Strobridge recognized the usefulness of the newfangled explosive, nitroglycerin, for blasting tunnels through hard rock. Because only small holes were needed for nitro, Strobridge saw that drilling time could be cut, and this new explosive's tremendous power could easily shatter the steely granite. But nitro was unpredictable, highly unstable and dangerous. The work went faster, but many lives were lost in the erratic explosions. Workers would pour the liquid into several holes drilled 15 to 18 inches deep in the rock. Then they would cap the holes with plugs and fire the explosive charges simultaneously with a slow match or a percussion cap. But sometimes not all the nitro would go off. The workers, unaware of the danger, would take picks and shovels to the face after the blast and begin clearing the debris. Many were blown to bits when a pick or crowbar accidentally hit an undetonated charge. In fact, Strobridge himself lost an eye in just such an accident. There might have been many more accidents, but the cold weather helped stabilize the volatile nitroglycerin.

Strangely enough, dynamite, which had been invented by this time and was much safer, was never used in building the tunnels of the Central Pacific. But Strobridge did find a way to save lives as well as money by having nitro manufactured on the spot at the sites of at least two of the CP's most challenging tunnels (called Tunnel No. 6, at the summit, and Tunnel No. 8). The cost was about 75 cents a pound, and excavation speed increased dramatically—with at least a 50 percent gain.

Finally, in late 1867, the Central Pacific crews finished the last of some 15 tunnels and dug their way out of the Sierra Nevada. For many, the "mountain job" had been the worst experience in their lives. One Irish crew boss, writing home to Pennsylvania, called his months at the summit "what Hell would be like if the blasted place really did freeze over." He promised to come home soon "and take that nice safe and quiet job" in a Philadelphia drugstore.

With the mountains behind them the Central Pacific crews began to speed eastward toward the Nevada desert. It had taken almost 41 months to lay tracks across the back-breaking range.

THE UNION PACIFIC, HEADING WEST

The rival Union Pacific, meanwhile, had a much easier time of it, challenged primarily by great, stretching expanses of prairie. Only four tunnels, a total length of 1,792 feet, had to be built along the entire length of the line. The UP was lucky enough to reach mountains that needed tunneling much later in its route, not beginning the first tunnel until 1868.

The railroad had laid 680 miles of track westward from Omaha, Nebraska before having to drive its first tunnel, Tunnel 1 on Mary's Creek in Rattlesnake Hills. In May and June 1868 the crews drove this short, straight tunnel, 215 feet long, through a spur of hills where the creek turned sharply. The rock was soft sandstone, easily excavated, especially in comparison to the rocky granite of the Sierra range, even though the UP crew of 150 Mormons included no experienced tunnel men at the time. But its soft walls and ceiling had to be lined with timber, which took nearly another two months. It was 19 feet wide where the arched roof began and 17 feet wide at the base. The clearance from rail to ceiling was only 20 feet 4 inches. In the tradition of the shooflies of the B&O Railroad, the Casement brothers, who were directing the track-laying crews, laid a sharply curving temporary track with many switchbacks around the hills so that progress could continue on the line while the tunnel was being built.

The longest tunnel on the line, Tunnel 2, 772 feet long, was built at Echo Canyon in the Wasatch Mountains of Utah. Begun in July 1868, this tunnel presented some problems. To lay track up to the tunnel site, the crews had to excavate deep approach cuts, and the tunnel had to be driven through much more solid rock. Hundreds of men, both Mormon and non-Mormon, labored on the excavation and at this point Sam Reed, who was in charge, brought in nitroglycerin to help with the job. At Julesburg, in Wyoming territory, a quickly built factory—a cabin insulated by dirt embankments in case of accident—supplied the oily explosive. The UP used nitro on this tunnel and the next (and probably on the fourth as well) with no serious accidents.

At Tunnel 2, a different problem faced the UP crews: an unstable clay that crumbled when exposed to air. Every hole the workers dug collapsed. Ideally,

the tunnelers would have used a masonry lining to stabilize the clay and hold the tunnel's roof and walls in place, but no cement or stone was available. At the time the work on the tunnel began, the head of the railroad was still 300 miles away, making transportation of supplies to the site very difficult. So the tunnel was lined with timber the tunnelers had on hand, a less-than-safe solution to the problem. And the crumbly clay continued to plague the workers as the excavation slowly progressed—so slowly, in fact, that the track layers, originally 300 miles away, approached closer and closer. Finally, they built an 8-mile temporary track around the site and passed on by. The tunnelers at Tunnel 2 kept on digging. They finally broke through in January 1869, but Tunnel 2 was not actually completed until after the Union Pacific and the Central Pacific met at Promontory Point, Utah in May of that year.

Meanwhile, Tunnel 3 and Tunnel 4 were begun in Weber Canyon, only ¾ of a mile from each other, 1,005 miles west of the UP's starting point in Omaha. Both tunnels were started in September 1868, but the 297-foot Tunnel 4 was finished first, in January 1869. Tunnel 3, chiseled 508 feet through black limestone and dark blue quartzite, took longer, and a sharply curving temporary track was laid so that the line could move on. Tunnel 3 was finally completed in April.

Like the Central Pacific, the Union Pacific had its challenges, which included severe blizzards, devastating floods and difficult gradings and bridges. In addition, the UP railroad company was faced with the challenge of fending off attacks by Native Americans hostile to the idea of ribbons of track and the iron horse running across their land. According to UP builder Grenville Dodge, "Our Indian troubles commenced in 1864 and lasted until the tracks joined at Promontory. . . . The order to every surveying corps, grading, bridging, and tie outfit was never to run when attacked. All were required to be armed . . ." These conditions made progress on the UP anything but easy. But the geological challenges faced by other railroad companies were far more demanding.

TUNNELING THROUGH THE CASCADES

A decade later, in the late 1870s, Henry Villard of the Northern Pacific and James Hill of the Great Northern began vying to complete the first northern transcontinental railroad route from Chicago through the

Major Railroad Tunnels in the United States

1833–1929

DATE	TUNNEL	LENGTH
1833	Allegheny Portage Tunnel (Staple Bend Tunnel) Begun in 1831, near Johnstown, Pennsylvania for the Allegheny Portage Railroad; first railroad tunnel in the United States (combined railroad and canal tunnel)	901 ft.
1876	Hoosac Tunnel Tunnel on the Troy and Greenfield Railroad in Massachusetts to complete the link between Troy, New York and north central Massachusetts	4.5 mi.
1890	Grand Trunk Tunnel Beneath the St. Claire River between Sarnia, Ontario in Canada and Port Huron, Michigan. First underwater railroad tunnel in America, built for the Grand Trunk Railroad	1 mi.
1900	Cascade Tunnel (first tunnel) Built for the Great Northern Railroad in Washington State and used by steam engines until 1909, when the railroad switched to electric locomotives to avoid ventilation problems	7.75 mi.
1904	East Boston Elevated Railway Tunnel Enabled trolley cars to travel from Maverick Square in East Boston under the harbor to the Court Street Station in Boston	1.4 mi.
1908	The Hudson Tubes Begun in 1874, the first major construction project to use compressed air (Hudson & Manhattan Railroad)	5,650 ft.
1910	Pennsylvania Railroad New York Tunnel Extension Extends PRR service from New Jersey to Manhattan beneath the Hudson River	15,600 ft.
	Pennsy East River Tubes The Long Island Railroad begins service from Manhattan under the East River	14,172 ft.
1928	Moffat Tunnel In Colorado, begun in 1923 for the Denver and Rio Grande Western Railway; 9,000 feet above sea level	6.2 mi.
	Musconetcong Tunnel On the Lehigh Valley Railroad; first use of dynamite on a big project	5,000 ft.
1929	Cascade Tunnel (second tunnel) In Washington State; begun in 1924, at 7.75 miles, the longest rail tunnel in North America; Great Northern Railroad	7.75 mi.

rugged Rocky Mountains and the Cascades in Washington State to Puget Sound on the coast.

Like Crocker, Villard hired huge crews of Chinese workers on the western end, with teams of Swedes and Irish working from the east, and succeeded in building 900 miles of railroad in two years. The route included 130 miles of heavy rock cutting, several trestles including one that was 1,800 feet long, and an impressive 3,850-foot tunnel through Mullan Pass. The tunnel was so hard to complete that a temporary bypass track was built around it—but its grade was so steep and its curves so sharp they were dubbed "outrageous." The tunnel cut 40 miles off the route, but until it was finally finished, the trains couldn't always

On the Burlington line in 1959, workers drive through bedrock to tunnel around the site of Boysen Dam on the Big Horn River in Wyoming. This tunnel is 7,131 feet long. American Association of Railroads

get through, as late as 1883 when the Northern Pacific was otherwise completed.

The Great Northern railroad company, in the meantime, also raced to connect East and West across the Pacific Northwest by a different route. Once built, tea and silk from the ports on Puget Sound, as well as Washington apples, grain, lumber and cattle were carried along it to eastern destinations. But the route was also not easy and the GN met some of its greatest construction challenges in the Cascades, where John F. Stevens, who would become the railroad's chief engineer, discovered a pass in 1889. In 1893, the Great Northern crossed what is now known as Stevens Pass by means of a complicated series of switchbacks. By 1900 the railroad had driven its first tunnel through below the pass to reduce the steep grades and sharp curves. The first Cascade Tunnel was 2.63 miles long and shortened the route by 9 miles. Problems with poisonous exhaust fumes and smoke plagued the tunnel, though. Steam engines struggling to make the 1-in-45 gradient (traveling only 45 feet horizontally for every foot gain in altitude—a very steep grade)

through the tunnel's length more than once left passengers nearly choked with sulfurous fumes. In 1909, after many near-tragedies, the Great Northern Railroad finally ran electricity through the tunnel so that electric locomotives replaced the steam engines on that part of the line.

Soon afterward Stevens began plans for a giant track relocation project to lower the grade and electrify 74 miles of the line between Wenatchee and Skykomish, Washington. The project included driving a tunnel through the mountain 500 feet down the slope from the 1900 Cascade Tunnel—this one an incredible 7.79 miles long! It was and still is the longest railroad tunnel in North America. Begun in 1924, the New Cascade Tunnel was completed in 1929.

TUNNELING THE GREAT DIVIDE

"Through the Rockies, Not Around Them" was the motto of the Denver and Rio Grande Western Railroad, and the railway did just that. But the Great Continental Divide required steep ascents to summits as high as 11,500 feet, with the track protected from avalanches by more than 2 miles of snow sheds. Dangerous curves made the route hazardous, and the grade was so steep that special locomotives had to be added, as many as five at a time, to haul the trains over the top. The going was slow, with trains at times moving only 7 mph. Only a great tunnel through would make the route viable. Originally envisioned by Denver Pacific Railroad builder David H. Moffat, the Moffat Tunnel could not actually be driven through the steely rock until many years after his death. By that time the location became part of the Denver and Salt Lake line, which in turn was absorbed into the D&RGW line.

After 10 years of negotiations with the City of Denver, the railroad and the city began a joint venture in 1923. The challenges of the terrain appeared similar to those presented by the 12⅓-mile Simplon Tunnel through the Alps, begun in 1898 and completed in 1906. So the Moffat engineers settled on a similar system of approach, driving a pilot tunnel parallel to the main tunnel, with connecting tunnels to the main heading for supply lines and ventilation.

Later, on the Moffat, the pilot tunnel would be broken out to provide the City of Denver with a water-supply tunnel. Driven 75 feet to the south of the main tunnel, the circular 12-foot water conduit was

A jumbo is a huge carriage on which drills are mounted. Usually traveling on tracks, it transports drills to the tunnel face and holds them in place for drilling. Courtesy of William Shank

7½ feet higher than the permanent grade of the railroad tunnel.

Begun in 1923, the project illustrated how far tunneling had come—not only in engineering savvy and equipment for burrowing through rock, but also in new-found concern for the risks taken by the crews. From the time camps and then towns were set up at the two portals early that year, the new emphasis was obvious. Both towns had hospitals, canteens and recreation facilities for the men, as well as sleeping huts accommodating two men in each room, with electric lights, laundry facilities and hot showers. Safety measures inside the tunnel became stressed as well. Crews wore oil slickers while working in the tunnel and were encouraged to protect themselves against the extreme damp and cold of the high-altitude location. Lights at the face were turned off and the men evacuated before each blasting session, and no one was

allowed to return to the face until the all-clear was given and the lights turned back on. Accidents, of course, still happened, but usually when the safety rules were ignored.

The pilot and the main tunnel were pushed ahead simultaneously, with the pilot a little ahead. This system worked out well. Drilling crews worked at the face of the main tunnel and then retreated through connecting tunnels to drill in the pilot tunnel while blasting was done. Finally the mucking crew took over to remove the debris in the main tunnel. Then the two crews would exchange places again.

Described as a "dull, low boom" according to Moffat Tunnel historian E. G. McMechen, for those inside the tunnel the blasting had a formidable effect:

A pulse-like quiver follows the first report; a curious, low, beating sound that seems to shake the walls and

Historical Headlines

1851–1890

1851   Bridge-building continues to improve: Wendell Bowman builds a new-design iron-truss bridge replacing Wernwag's across the Potomac at Harpers Ferry.

1852   Albert Fink builds a truss bridge for the B&O Railroad over the Monongahela River at Fairmont, Virginia.

1853   As westward movement continues, Congress authorizes a survey for transcontinental railroad.

The United States purchases 30,000 square miles now located in Arizona and New Mexico from Mexico (Gadsden Purchase) for $10 million, adding the last territories currently forming the contiguous United States.

1854   The Republican Party is founded, championing, among other causes, a transcontinental railroad.

1855   Railroad suspension bridge completed at Niagara Falls by John Roebling.

Proslavery and abolitionist factions battle in Kansas until peace is restored by federal troops in 1856.

1857   The Dred Scott decision by U.S. Supreme Court declares the Missouri Compromise unconstitutional and holds that living in free territory does not make a slave free.

1860   Abraham Lincoln elected president.

South Carolina secedes from the Union, joined the following year by Mississippi, Florida, Alabama, Georgia, Louisiana, Texas, Virginia, Arkansas, North Carolina and Tennessee, when these 11 states form the Confederate States of America.

1861   April 12. Confederates fire on Fort Sumter, South Carolina, and the Civil War begins.

1862   Pacific Railway Act gives authority to Union Pacific Railroad to build westward from Nebraska to Utah to meet the Central Pacific, which is building eastward from California.

1864   Lincoln is elected president.

1865   Civil War ends; over the next few years the secessionist states are readmitted to the Union.

Lincoln is killed by John Wilkes Booth; Vice President Andrew Johnson becomes president.

Thirteenth Amendment to the Constitution abolishing slavery is ratified by 27 states.

1867   Albert Fink builds a truss railroad bridge across thye Ohio River to Louisville, Kentucky.

The United States buys Alaska from Russia for $7.2 million.

1869   May 10. The first transcontinental railroad is completed at Promontory Point, Utah.

Wyoming Territory gives women the right to vote

1871   The first Ohio River railroad crossing is built, an iron and wood truss between Bellaire, Ohio, and Benwood, West Virginia.

1874   St. Louis Bridge (later renamed the Eads Bridge) is completed, the first to cross the Mississippi. A railroad bridge, it is the first major steel construction in the United States.

1876   Collapsing railroad bridges begin to become a serious problem: 80 people die and 35 more are injured in railroad bridge collapse at Ashtabula Creek in Ohio.

1878   Philadelphia installs electric arc lights.

1880   United States population has swelled to 50.1 million.

1883   Brooklyn Bridge, largest suspension bridge in the world up to this time, is completed.

1888   After 17 years of discussion and construction, the Poughkeepsie Bridge (a railroad bridge), is completed across the Hudson River in upstate New York.

1889   Expansion continues: Oklahoma Territory (previously Indian Territory) opened to white settlers.

the ground beneath the feet as tho a seismic disturbance has occurred. The fluttering vibration enters the human body, throbs through the veins . . . Another explosion follows—another—another—irregular in time, seemingly interminable in duration.

The progress did not proceed smoothly. As often happened, especially in early tunnels, the geological survey had not revealed many of the problems that the tunnelers discovered as they blasted away at the mountain rock. A lake 1,100 feet above the tunnel heading on the east side began leaking into the tunnel. The crews sealed off the fissure with cement and continued to work. But in February 1926 the ground at the east heading suddenly heaved before the mucking crew after a blast. A deluge of water poured into the cavern. The men ran. Behind them the jumbo (a huge carriage mounted with drills) and mucking machine sat submerged in water while 3,100 gallons a minute flowed into the tunnel for six days. Finally the gush of water slowed and, with two pumps working, control seemed in sight, when a violent blizzard blew up at the east portal, snapping the power lines with its winds. The pumps stopped and the tunnel filled up again. By the time power was restored 10 minutes later, water was running out of the east portal. Then just as things were almost under control again, another power failure occurred and flooded the heading again. In all, work came to a standstill in the railroad tunnel for three full months.

Meanwhile, on the west side, where the geologists had anticipated hard rock, the rock turned out to be full of faults trickling with water. The problem was severe; the ground was so saturated that it ran. In fact,

the engineers were stumped until general manager George Lewis came up with an invention that came to be called the Lewis Girder. Working on the same principle as the English method of crown bars, the girder was an immensely strong bar that was cantilevered out from the completed tunnel to support the roof weight and hold wall plates in place until the tunnel beneath it could be fully excavated and lined. Then the 65-foot, 3½-foot thick bar was moved forward in a top pilot heading to hold up the next 20 feet of roof while the section below was removed.

In all, the tunneling crews not only struggled against what seemed, as McMechen put it, "an intelligent and malignant force within . . . the mountain," but also the tunnel required nearly three and a half miles of timbering where the estimators had anticipated only 1,500 feet of timbering.

The Moffat Tunnel took five solid years of work, night and day, to complete. The 6⅕-mile bore enabled the D&RGW line to trim 173 miles off its route, providing a short-cut under James Peak in the Rocky Mountains in Colorado. The job cost $16 million and the first train rolled through on February 27, 1928. In 1934, a cutoff was added enabling the D&RGW to connect with the Denver & Salt Lake line through the Moffat Tunnel, running its trains directly from Denver to Salt Lake City, Utah.

Meanwhile, as crews had been toiling in the cold, rocky mountains of the West, in the East, New York City had wrestled with enormous transportation problems of its own. It proved to be another site where breakthroughs in tunneling technology—including Charles Burleigh's drill—were contributing answers to the problem of getting from here to there.

6

"TO HARLEM IN 15 MINUTES": THE NEW YORK CITY SUBWAY

Anyone who ventures into the pulsing, grinding traffic of New York City today knows that getting around in Manhattan requires a vast measure of patience and perseverance. What might surprise most people is that 125 years ago the streets of New York were nearly as congested and the city's citizens almost as close to running out of patience as they are today. The tiny island of Manhattan, the heart of New York City, measures only 22 square miles and by 1855 was home to some 700,000 people. As described by the New York Evening Post in the 1860s:

> New York has already nearly a million inhabitants, miserably accommodated for the most part . . . At present it is the most inconveniently arranged commercial city in the world. Its wharves are badly built, unsafe, and without shelter; its streets are badly paved, dirty and miserably overcrowded . . . The means of going from one part of the city to the other are so badly contrived that a considerable part of the working population . . . spends a sixth of their working day on the street cars or omnibuses.

In fact, in 1867, a reporter for the New York Tribune counted 13,391 vehicles in one 13-hour period, as he observed the passing traffic from a vantage point on Broadway.

ELY BEACH AND THE PNEUMATIC UNDERGROUND

But no easy solution was in sight. The omnibus service proprietors were in cahoots with "Boss" Tweed, the notoriously corrupt New York City political boss. He protected their business from competition, and they paid him a slice of their handsome profits. As a result, Tweed maintained a veritable lock on the city's transit services. In short, Tweed was able to block any legislation at the state capitol that might threaten his tidy transit empire. This was the case until Alfred Ely Beach, who served as editor of the New York *Sun* newspaper, as well as the newly started *Scientific American*, figured out a way around Tweed's hold on the city's transit system.

Beach possessed a large dose of "can-do" spirit, and he patented several inventions of his own. He became fascinated with the idea of pneumatic tube railways, which English and French engineers had been experimenting with since about 1844. In 1867 he demonstrated his own working model at the Exhibition of the American Institute at the Fourteenth Street Armory. His model consisted of a wooden tube, 6 feet in diameter, 1 inch larger than the passenger car within, with a fan driven by a stationary steam engine at one end. Air blowing through the tube propelled the car,

The tunnel shield invented by Marc Isambard Brunel to hold the silt back while digging under the Thames River in London. From a contemporary drawing

and its passengers, 107 feet to the other end of the tube. Beach's demonstration was a phenomenal success, with 100,000 delighted passengers taking the ride.

"The ponderous locomotive," Beach explained in a booklet he published shortly afterward, "is dispensed with, and the light airial fluid that we breathe is the substituted motor."

Beach had become convinced that a pneumatic train, either elevated or subway, was the only logical way to solve the city's transit problems, and he thought the public would back the idea if only a convincing demonstration could be made. Obviously, it was not in "Boss" Tweed's interest to let such a demonstration take place. So Beach applied to the state legislature for a charter to build a set of pneumatic mail delivery tubes, 4½ feet in diameter, underground between Warren and Cedar streets near Broadway. Clearly not large enough for a transportation system, the tubes were approved with no opposition from Tweed and his lobbyists. Beach then cleverly got tacked on to his charter an amendment transforming the two small tubes into one large tube. Miraculously he was able to sneak his modification past

Tweed's supporters in 1868 and win approval to start building.

Later that same year, Beach's crews set to work beneath the street, using a special hydraulic shield designed by Beach himself. Similar to a device invented by Marc Isambard Brunel in 1818 for use tunneling beneath the Thames, Beach's shield, however, was a cylinder, "which resembled a barrel with the ends out." In this respect Beach's shield foreshadowed the Greathead shield, first used in 1869 and perfected in 1880 (see box in Chapter 7), which was a major breakthrough for underwater tunneling and became the standard in the industry.

Six men formed the crew on the Beach subway. Two men worked the hydraulic rams of the shield, which shoved the cutting edges of the eight horizontal shelves forward with amazing precision. Two more men mucked out, removing the debris that had been loosened. And the last two followed up behind, under the protection of the shield's hood, laying the brick of the lining.

Only one obstacle slowed the progress toward completion of the 312-foot tunnel through the soft soil— an old Dutch fort buried beneath the street. Beach and his workers decided that the best thing to do was to put their shield to the test and dig right through the walls of the fort. The shield held as the crew removed the fort's stones from their path one by one, and progress on the tunnel continued. The job was finished in 58 days.

Curiously enough, the tunnel was built in total secrecy in the stealth of the night. Beginning from the basement of a clothing store at Warren Street and Broadway, Beach's crews operated under the cover of darkness, even muffling the wheels of the wagons, which were covered to avoid suspicion as they carried away tons of debris that were excavated. The objective: to avoid arousing Tweed's suspicions.

It worked. The finished tunnel was a showpiece, long and straight, with a single sweeping curve at the Warren Street Station. The tunnel's cylindrical walls of brick were painted an airy white and lit by gaslight and Zircon oxygen lamps, the latest in illumination. And hidden from sight, the "Western Tornado," a giant, 100-horsepower fan weighing 50 tons, propelled the single passenger car along the track with a quiet "whoosh."

Beach's subway created a sensation, and for a while it looked like he would succeed in building a transit system for all of New York City. But the financial instability caused by the Panic of 1873 ended his prospects and instead the future of New York transportation veered off in another direction: the elevated train.

NEW YORK TRIES TRAINS ON STILTS

The idea of the elevated train took hold of New York City, despite another attempt by Boss Tweed to avert competition, and 37½ miles of "els" were built. The consequences were less than happy. Many of the once broad, open streets of the city now lurked in the shadows of these second-story trains, or "bridges." Ten years after their completion, in 1890, Philadelphia engineer John J. Derry gave this summary of the New York el system:

> The El system obstructs light, privacy, and air; is a nuisance from constant noise and drippings from the structure in inclement weather; the traffic is delayed by fogs, windstorms, snow, slippery rails and fires; it practically absorbs a street for structure and the cars and engines pass within 8 or 12 feet of house lines; it is a nuisance from cinders, smoke and dripping grease, produces injury to the eyes of pedestrians from constant falling of steel filings from the grinding of car-wheels on rails, obliterates each street section where stations are located; and the length of the train and capacity can never be extended beyond the limit of the strength of the structure.

As if these objections were not bad enough, the el didn't solve the city's transportation problems, either. As one writer for the New York *Evening Post* put it in 1885: "As for comfortable city travel, we are back in the old days when the city had outgrown the streetcar system and as yet even the elevated roads were not. The daily journeys up and down have again become times of dread and seasons of anguish." The density of population was greater and the trains more crowded than ever. An estimated 60,831,757 people traveled on 32½ miles of el track in 1880 and 10 years later, 188,203,877 passengers traveled along the same route.

The idea of a subway, meanwhile, was still percolating in the minds of some. In fact, a project called the

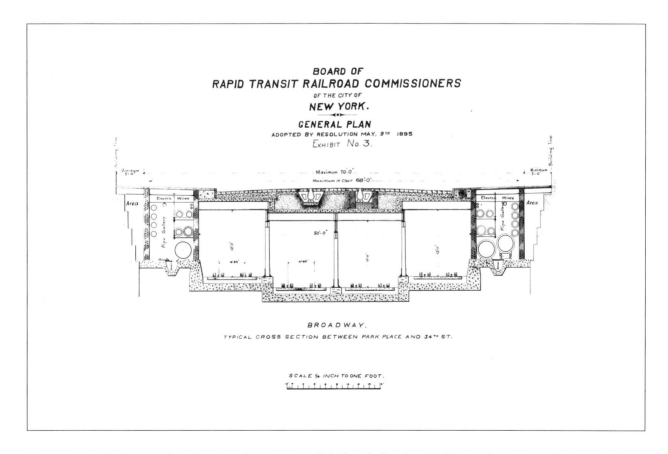

A cross section of the New York City subway tunnel as it was actually built under Broadway. In this part of the tunnel, built using cut-and-cover construction, utility tunnels ran on the outside, with four-track tunnels in the center. Courtesy of New York Transit Museum Archives

Arcade Railway—a subway beneath Broadway—was conceived in 1866. Intended to be not only a transportation system but a sort of great underground mall, the Arcade's proponents wanted "not merely to tunnel the street, but to remove the street itself, block by block, from wall to wall, and construct another street below supporting the present street on arches, turning what are now basements and sub-basements into stores." Light would come through translucent glass in the sidewalks above, with fresh air flowing in through sidewalk vents. A promenade would run on either side of the Arcade's four railroad tracks. For 19 years this idea was toyed with, until finally, concerned about its shortcomings—particularly the inadequate plans for ventilation—engineer William Barclay Parsons and others broke off from the project and formed the New York District Railway in 1885.

By this time Beach's demonstration was a dim memory of the past and the el system was emerging as a giant mistake. The New York District Railway claimed it could offer a new, "scientific street" that could measure up to "all the demands which modern civilization has created." Its cars would be made of a wonderful new fiber called "Ferflax," a sort of iron cloth, "compounded of steel wire netting, vegetable fiber, and oxidized oil compressed into a solid panel by hydraulic power."

FINALLY A SUBWAY

Both the Arcade and the New York District Railway projects ended in nothing, however. Finally, by 1894, the transit situation in New York City had become unbearable. One billion passengers traveled the city's surface railroads and els each year, and each year that number increased by 6 to 7 percent. The Rapid Transit Commission was re-assembled and Barclay Parsons appointed as chief engineer. He was 35 and on the brink of the greatest project of his life: the New York City subway system.

Financial problems had to be worked out first, though, and construction did not begin until March 24, 1900. By this time many of the world's major cities—including London, Paris, Boston and even Glasgow, Scotland and Budapest, Hungary—already had subway transit systems in full operation. The New

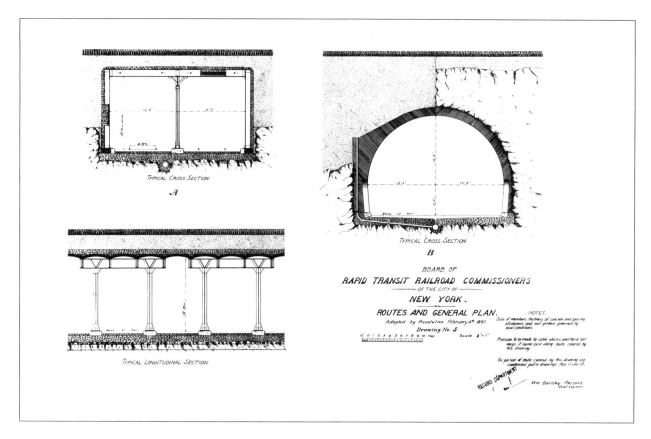

Plans for the New York City subway showing two tunnel cross sections and a longitudinal, or side, view. Courtesy of New York Transit Museum Archives

Work progressing beneath the streets of New York City in 1901. Courtesy of New York Transit Museum Archives

York press was jubilant at first, with the New York *World* hyping the subway as capable of taking its passengers "to Harlem in Fifteen Minutes."

Parsons, however, was more realistic. "For New York," he wrote in May 1900, "there is no such thing as a solution to the Rapid Transit problem . . . By the time the railway is completed, areas that are now given over to rocks and goats will be covered with houses, and there will be created for each new line . . . a special traffic of its own, independent of the normal growth of the city." He was, of course, right. But the work was begun.

Most of the work was done using the "cut-and-cover" method of tunnel construction. That is, the streets were torn up and the old pipes and sewers relocated. A rectangular tunnel was then constructed complete with tracks, and, finally, the street pavement was replaced overhead. At Murray Hill, however, the subway was tunneled beneath the Park Avenue trolley tunnel. There, the workers hung the sewage and water pipes by chains from a wooden framework while they blasted through the rock beneath.

Dynamite was also required at Fort George, below Washington Heights, in upper Manhattan. Here, the workers sank four vertical shafts, one at 157th Street, another at 195th Street, and two more in between. From these they burrowed secondary headings to complete a 2-mile tunnel 125 feet below the crest of the hill. At the time, it was the longest two-track tunnel in the United States.

Even though the cut-and-cover method Parsons chose for most of the subway played havoc with the New York City street traffic during construction, he maintained that the advantages outweighed the temporary inconvenience. This method enabled most of the subway to be built less than 14 feet below the surface, which meant there would be few stairs and passengers could get to the stations easily. In addition, many of the stations could be lit during daylight hours, with sunlight through glass in the sidewalks—offsetting, he said, "the popular antipathy to a 'hole in the ground.'"

From 1900 to 1904 as construction continued, however, the chaos proved overwhelming. As one writer reported at the time, "The whole place was a great chasm. Business in the neighborhood went to ruin. Crowds hurrying to the Grand Central [railroad] Terminal passed rows of empty houses, from which store-

Streets were torn up and topside traffic came to a halt during the cut-and-cover construction on the New York City subway between 1900 and 1904. Courtesy of New York Transit Museum Archives

Digging at Fort George in 1904. Courtesy of New York Transit Museum Archives

keepers and other occupants had fled as from the plague. The neighborhood of City Hall, too, resembled a cross between a mining camp and a mound dwellers' colony."

The construction crews also encountered innumerable problems. Thousands of workers suffered injuries or were maimed in accidents. Many—between 50 and 120—were killed. A steam boiler crushed one victim at 64th Street and Broadway. A rock fall killed five more at 164th Street. At 42nd Street and Park Avenue, seven men were killed and 180 more injured when an entire shack full of dynamite blew up—a worker taking his lunch break in the shack had innocently lit a candle to warm up a little. After a blast at 145th Street and St. Nicholas Avenue near Fort George, a whole crew of men were killed when a delayed charge went off as they headed back to work to muck out the heading.

Beneath the teeming city, odd things—mastadon bones and buried ponds—were found, too. A charred hull of a Dutch merchant ship that had sunk in 1613 was uncovered as well as old coins and colonial relics. Workers also came across Alfred Ely Beach's pneumatic subway, already all but forgotten.

The first eight-car New York City Subway train operated over 9.1 miles of track on October 27, 1904, and in that first year it carried 383.7 million passengers. Further extensions were added rapidly. In 1905, a 650-foot tunnel was added across the Harlem River to the Bronx. Tubes for the tunnel were constructed on dry land in an early version of the "immersed-tube" method of underwater tunneling widely used for much larger tunnels today. Sealed watertight, the tubes were then encased in a covering of iron and concrete and sunk to the river bottom, where workers bolted them to the tunnel headings on both sides of the river.

In 1908, a 5,385-foot-long tunnel under the East River connected the subway with Brooklyn at Joralemon Street. In 1911, ground was broken at 62nd Street and Lexington Avenue to begin the Lexington Avenue line. And in 1915, the 3,500-foot-long Steinway tunnel was added under the East River, to Queens.

Passengers rushing to board and exit from a train stopped at the Bowling Green Station, one of the New York City subway's newest stations. Courtesy of New York City Transit Authority

Today the New York City Subway system, run by the New York City Transit Authority, transports some 3.7 million passengers each weekday—720,000 during the hours of 7:00 A.M. to 9:30 A.M. alone. It runs 860

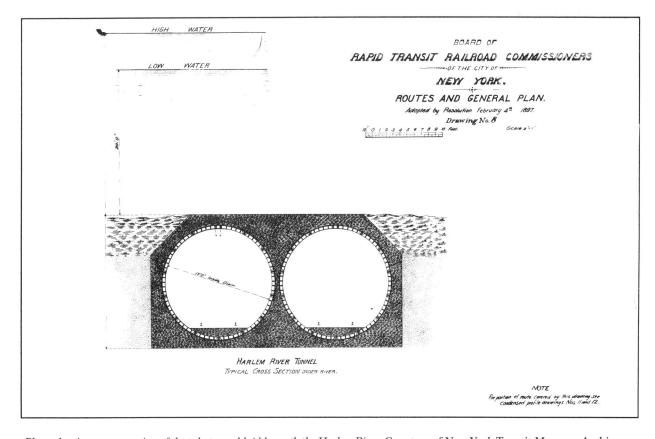

Plans showing a cross section of the tube tunnel laid beneath the Harlem River. Courtesy of New York Transit Museum Archives

Train idling at the 21st Street Station, Long Island City, Queens. Courtesy of New York City Transit Authority

trains during the morning weekday rush hours, making 6,500 daily train trips over 722 miles of track.

And New Yorkers still have plans for its expansion, though today more slowly than ever. In October 1989 a new extension running beneath the East River to Roosevelt Island and Queens was completed at 63rd Street. First conceived 20 years earlier, the subway line extension was long known as the "Subway to Nowhere" by its critics—when completed, it extended only 3.2 miles and stopped short of major connections to other lines. It cost $868 million to build and carries some 13,500 commuters a day.

Other plans for addition of 11 subway lines and a new tunnel for the Long Island Railroad have long been stymied by fiscal crises, structural problems and neighborhood protests. The subway's detractors are vocal and visible—whether crowded or deserted, subway platforms and trains seem to invite crime. But tunneling beneath the teeming streets still appears, today as much as 100 years ago, to be a viable method to bypass Manhattan's pressing traffic problems.

Historical Headlines

1891–1904

1892   In Chicago, the first electric automobile (made by William Morrison of Des Moines, Iowa) is driven.

Frank and Charles Duryea of Massachusetts make the first American gasoline automobile.

1894   German inventor Rudolf Diesel invents the Diesel engine.

1898   Spanish-American War begins; the Treaty of Paris is signed in December with the United States emerging as a recognized world power.

McKinley takes a ride in a Stanley Steamer, becoming the first president to ride in an automobile.

1903   A Packard car travels from San Francisco to New York in 52 days in the first trip across the United States by automobile.

Henry Ford establishes the Ford Motor Company.

Orville and Wilbur Wright make the first successful manned flight of a motorized aircraft at Kitty Hawk, North Carolina, on December 17.

The Williamsburg Bridge, over the East River in New York City, becomes the first large suspension bridge to be constructed using steel towers.

7

UNDERWATER BREAKTHROUGH: TUNNELING UNDER NEW YORK'S RIVERS

New York City became a major port and commercial center as early as 1700, and yet, the city's major asset—its harbor—also created one of its major transportation problems. The heart of New York City, Manhattan Island, is bordered on the east by the East River and on the west by the mighty Hudson. To connect Manhattan with the mainland, ferry lines began making regular runs as far back as the 1700s. The Hoboken Ferry, which wasn't the first, began making its way across the Hudson between Manhattan and Hoboken, New Jersey in 1775. By the 19th century, as reliance on the railroads increased, the railroad and ferries coordinated schedules so passengers and freight could make the connections between the mainland and Manhattan. In fact, some of the railroads even annexed the old ferry lines. The Hoboken Ferry, for example, became a subsidiary of the Delaware, Lackawanna and Western Railroad.

By 1860, New York City's population had swelled to more than a million—and yet, anyone crossing the Hudson from New Jersey or the East River from Brooklyn or the rest of Long Island still had to make the slow trip by ferry. In winter, the ferries often became trapped in the ice and the only crossing possible was over the ice on foot.

At the time, no bridge crossed either the Hudson or the East River (the Brooklyn Bridge was not even begun until 1869 and took 14 years to build). And no plans existed for building railroad bridges in any case. A bridge had to be built high enough above the harbor so it would not block the passage of ships and boats—and such a bridge required either steep approaches or longer, more gradual ascents. But railroad locomotives weren't powerful enough in the 1860s to climb steep approaches. And longer approaches with grades low enough for the locomotives would eat up too much of Manhattan's already crowded terrain.

So the idea of tunneling underneath New York's rivers teased the imaginations of both the sane and the less than sane. One visionary known as "Crazy Luke," so the story goes, used to stop Wall Street financiers on their way to lunch to harangue for money to finance his dream of a mile-long tunnel under the Hudson. Although Luke finally wound up in an asylum, others went on to prove that his idea had merit.

HASKIN'S HASSLE

While Leonardo da Vinci had sketched equipment for building an underwater tunnel in the 15th century, no one had really tunneled underwater successfully for any great distance when DeWitt Clinton Haskin began his "Hudson Tubes" project in 1874. (Marc Brunel's tunnel under the Thames in London, com-

47

Major Underwater Tunnels in the United States

1870–1957*

DATE	TUNNEL	LENGTH
1870	Washington Street Tunnel Beneath the Chicago River in Chicago, the first tunnel built for vehicles in the United States, with two passageways, one for horse-drawn vehicles and another for foot traffic	1,608 ft. (vehicular tube) 810 ft. (pedestrian tube)
1890	Grand Trunk Tunnel Beneath the St. Claire River between Sarnia, Ontario in Canada and Port Huron, Michigan. First underwater railroad tunnel in America, built for the Grand Trunk Railroad	1 mi.
1904	East Boston Tunnel Enabled trolley cars to travel from Maverick Square in East Boston under the harbor to the Court Street station in Boston	1.4 mi.
1908	The Hudson Tubes Begun in 1874 between New Jersey and Manhattan, the first major construction project to use compressed air	5,650 ft.
1927	Holland Tunnel First auto tunnel to solve the ventilation problem with a fresh-air system	8,556 ft. (north tube) 8,371 ft. (south tube)
1928	George A. Posey Tube Connecting Oakland, California, with the island city of Alameda. Early use of the immersed-tube method of construction	3,545 ft.
1937, 1945, 1957	Lincoln Tunnel Three-tube tunnel beneath the Hudson River, connecting New York and New Jersey	8,216 feet (central tube) 7,482 ft. (north tube) 8,006 ft. (south tube)
1940	Queens Tunnel First road tunnel under the East River, connecting Manhattan and Queens	6,414 ft.
1941	Bankhead Tunnel Crosses beneath the Mobile River in Mobile, Alabama	3,109 ft.
1950	Brooklyn-Battery Tunnel Connects Brooklyn with Lower Manhattan beneath the East River	9,117 ft.
1957	Baltimore Harbor Tunnel In Maryland, beneath Baltimore Harbor, one of the world's longest twin-tube underwater tunnels	7,650 ft.

* For more underwater tunnels, see "Immersed-Tube Tunnels" in Chapter 9

pleted in 1843, was only 1,506 feet long.) Haskin, a Californian who had recently traveled in the Midwest, had seen a bridge across the Missouri under construction at Omaha, Nebraska. There, he had seen how caissons were being used to sink the great bridge piers down to bedrock below the waters of the Missouri (a method used by James Eads between 1867 and 1874 in building the St. Louis Bridge across the Mississippi). A caisson is a big, open-ended box inverted over the river bottom. Compressed air was pumped into the box to provide atmosphere beneath the water for workers whose job it was to scoop the muck—rocks and mud—from the river bottom. Meanwhile, the edges of the caisson kept pushing down as the bottom inside was scooped out and hauled up to the surface. To Haskins, this seemed a solution to the Hudson River tunnel problem, as well. He believed he could use the same techniques he had seen in Nebraska to push aside the Hudson River's soft silt river bottom for a pair of tubes to carry a railroad.

So in 1873, having obtained $10 million in financing from a man named Trevor Park, he founded the Hudson Tunnel Railroad Company. With work begun in November 1874, the western shaft was nearly completed that year and Haskins's workers were about ready to begin digging the tunnel from the Jersey side. But the progress didn't continue long. On December 15, the Delaware, Lackawanna and Western Railroad—which operated a ferry across the Hudson—brought an injunction against Haskins's company for invading its territory on the New Jersey shore. All the work on the tunnel came to a grinding halt. For the next five years, until the conflict was settled, no further progress was made.

Finally, the railway company's suit was defeated and, in September 1879, the digging began on the tunnel. However, Haskins's troubles had not come to an end. While he wisely thought of using pressurized air at 35 pounds per square inch inside his "caisson," he overlooked one important point: His caisson, unlike those used on the river in Omaha, lay on its side, its open end not more than 15 feet below the unforgiving waters of the Hudson. (In bridge construction the open end faces downward, toward bedrock.) But Haskins's sandhogs shoveled muck without a shield between them and the soft silt. On July 21, 1880, as tunneling reached an area of the river bottom that was less stable, the pressure inside the

tunnel—which was greater than the air pressure above—suddenly began to whoosh out.

Typically such blowouts almost always caused deaths among the sandhogs working inside a tunnel, with the sudden change in air pressure and the influx of mud and water. Sometimes workers were sucked out of the tunnel to the surface of the water (and occasionally a few lived to tell about it). In this case, the workers realized a blowout was about to occur and began running for the pressurized door to safety. Some escaped, thanks to the quick thinking and heroism of one worker named Peter Woodland. As he reached the door, he realized there wasn't time for everyone to make it out—and if the door was not closed everyone would die, even those already on the other side. Woodland closed the door and lost his life, along with the 19 others behind him. Thanks to him, however, the rest escaped.

After further technical and financial disasters, Haskins finally had to abandon the project. Even if Haskins had managed to finish the tubes, his plan to send steam locomotives through the tunnel, exiting at a terminal near Washington Square, was not well thought through. He didn't consider the fact that, without ventilation in the tunnel, smoke from the engines would have asphyxiated passengers and crews as it did in the Great Northern's first Cascade Tunnel. However, despite his unsuccessful attempt, Haskins had advanced the beginnings of a tunnel, lined with brick, extending 1,200 feet from the New Jersey shore.

PEARSON BRINGS IN THE GREATHEAD SHIELD

In 1888, a firm called the Hudson River Tunnel Company, backed by British financing, pushed the Haskins tube another 1,600 feet—almost to the Manhattan shore. They also started a second tube parallel to the first. The contractor, S. Pearson and Sons, was a knowledgeable and experienced team that had also built the Bridge of Forth in Scotland. Instead of Haskins's brick and mortar, Pearson used cast iron rings ("iron segmental linings") to build the tunnel's tube. But, most important of all, Pearson brought in the Greathead Shield. Originally designed by Peter Barlow and perfected by Sir James Henry Greathead, a South African–born British engineer, the shield was initially used on the Tower Subway in London in 1880.

Holding Back Water and Silt:
Shields and Compressed Air

DeWitt Clinton Haskins was the first to use compressed air to hold back water in any U.S. tunneling project, although the technique was also used by James Eads in sinking piers for a bridge across the Mississippi at St. Louis. Seeping water was usually a big problem when tunneling in soft ground, especially, of course, under water. Haskins realized, however, that by increasing the air pressure in a tunnel, he could hold the water back. Workers could enter and leave the working area through an air lock.

In principle, if the air pressure is as great as the pressure of water trying to fill the hole, then the water stops flowing in. But the two pressures must be exactly the same. If the air pressure is too great, air will push through any weakness in the surrounding ground to the surface—forming a hole in the riverbed. The air gushes out and water immediately surges through the hole to flood the tunnel chamber, usually killing the tunnelers in this disastrous phenomenon known as a "blowout."

French tunneler Marc Brunel, British bridge and tunnel builder Peter William Barlow and South African engineer James H. Greathead were the first to devise another approach to the problem—shields erected at the tunnel face. These shields greatly increased the speed and safety of tunneling underwater. Brunel, who patented his first shield in 1818, began tunneling with another version of his shield beneath the Thames River in London in 1825. Brunel's invention fitted the shape of the tunnel's cross-section at the face and held back the ooze of the silt, while workers dug out the muck.

The shield was made of 12 narrow cast-iron frames 22 feet high, together weighing 80 tons. Each frame, less than 3 feet wide, contained three platforms, one above the other, where the sandhogs worked. These workers carefully removed boards at the front of the shield, one by one, dug out the muck from behind and then replaced the boards at the new forward position. Others carried the muck away and still others laid mortar and bricks to extend the tunnel lining forward behind the shield. To move the shield forward as the muck in front was removed, workers turned jackscrews braced between the new front edge of the lining and the shield. The system worked, but the tunneling progressed very slowly. It took Brunel and his crews 18 years to complete the project, after many mishaps and setbacks.

In 1869, Barlow and 25-year-old Greathead started a second tunnel under the Thames. For this tunnel they used an iron shield, circular in shape, known as the Greathead Shield, although Barlow, the more experienced engineer, actually invented the first version. This shield was not just bracing, as Brunel's model had been. It was a great cylinder of iron, with a cutting edge around the circumference, like a giant cookie cutter. Between the shield and the tunnel face Barlow and Greathead used compressed air to help keep the water out. They also introduced the use of prefabricated cast-iron segments for the tunnel lining instead of brick, a system used later, under the Hudson, by Pearson. In less than a year Barlow and Greathead's tunnel under the Thames was completed. In the United States, meanwhile, for his short subway tunnel under Broadway in New York, Alfred Ely Beach invented a shield of his own design at about the same time.

DeWitt Clinton Haskins, however, decided to try tunneling beneath the Hudson without a shield. It was a decision he would come to regret.

Charles M. Jacobs, with his East River Gas Tunnel (1892–94), was the first to bring the three tunneling principles together: compressed air to keep the water back, an air lock for workers to come and go through, and the Greathead shield. He and William McAdoo set those principles to work to complete Haskins's Hudson Tubes, finally, with the first train running through in 1908.

Workers inside the shield at the Holland Tunnel face during construction. Most shields used in underwater construction were patterned after the Greathead shield. Courtesy of Port Authority of New York and New Jersey

Alfred Ely Beach, of course, had already used a shield of his own design to build his pneumatic subway beneath Broadway in 1870. But by 1888, Beach's little subway, and its shield, had already drifted out of most people's memories. The principle, however, was the same: a cylinder of iron having a forward cutting edge, slightly tapered toward the back to reduce friction with the surrounding soil. The lining of the tunnel had a slightly smaller diameter than the shield so that it could actually be constructed safely inside the shield. Then the shield was shoved forward by jacks—screw-jacks in the case of the Greathead model—braced against the completed edge of the lining. The shield provided the critical advantage of a closed end—so important in underwater tunneling—to prevent the outrush of compressed air through weaknesses in the river bottom and the inrush of water. With the risk of pressure failure in the tubes greatly reduced, the work progressed much faster and more safely.

But the Hudson River Tunnel Company also ran out of money, with 3,700 feet of tunnel completed, and in mid-1891 work again came to a halt. About $3 million into the job, Pearson had to give up, only

Railway cars (here filled with men posing for the camera) were used to remove rock and muck from beneath the Hudson. Courtesy of Port Authority of New York and New Jersey

Deep Tunneling vs. the Human Body: Battling the Bends

Up until 1889 the dread disease known as "the bends" took the lives of one out of every four workers who labored inside a pressure lock. But advances in medical knowledge helped give sandhogs working on McAdoo's tunnel beneath the Hudson River a much better chance—even though they were working under pressure amounting to 38 pounds per square inch, much higher than the normal atmospheric air pressure of 14.69 pounds per square inch.

What medical scientists finally discovered in 1889 is that fatalities and crippling were caused by transferring too quickly—returning to normal air pressure or vice versa. This sudden change creates an excess of nitrogen molecules in the bloodstream. If, however, the workers returned to normal pressure carefully and slowly, it was discovered, they could avoid the bends altogether.

By using a rate of decompression equal to one minute for every two pounds of pressure, workers on McAdoo's tunnel beneath the Hudson had far fewer problems. For sandhogs who did show signs of the bends, a "hospital lock" was constructed near the tunnel shaft. There, the ailing worker would be placed again under higher pressure and decompressed at an even slower, more careful rate.

By the time crews were working in the 46-pound pressure of the Lincoln Tunnel South Tube in the 1950s, even greater safety measures were taken, with crews working only 30 minutes at a time, followed by long, six-hour rest periods.

$650,000 short. The remaining 1,600 feet would be completed by another man, William Gibbs McAdoo.

MCADOO AND THE PENNSYLVANIA RAILROAD

"The Fates had marked a day," wrote William McAdoo, "when I was to go under the riverbed and encounter this piece of dripping darkness, and it would rise from its grave and walk by my side. I was destined to give it color and movement and warmth, but it would change the course of my life and lead me into a new career."

McAdoo arrived in New York in 1892 at the age of 28. Georgia-born, he had become a deputy clerk in the U.S. circuit court in Chattanooga at the age of 19, studied law in Tennessee, and attempted an unsuccessful reorganization of the Knoxville street railway system. A man whose extraordinary intensity and vigor showed in his face, McAdoo was destined to leave his mark on the New York transportation system. For he was the man who would finish the Hudson Tubes—and much more.

In 1901, McAdoo began to think seriously about the problem of tunneling under the Hudson—but he didn't know anyone had ever tried it until he was talking one day with John Dos Passos (a lawyer, not the writer), who told him about the earlier attempts.

Shortly thereafter he met Charles M. Jacobs, the engineer who had constructed the first underwater tunnel in New York. Although Jacobs's tunnel was only 8 feet wide, built for gas mains under the East River in 1894, many of the challenges were the same. In October 1901, wearing yellow slickers and hip boots, McAdoo and Jacobs took the trip down the abandoned shaft Haskins had built on the New Jersey side and walked into the tunnel excavation. McAdoo would later describe this experience as his descent into "this dripping darkness."

Together the two men walked about 2,800 feet to the Greathead Shield left behind by Pearson. It was still usable, in Jacobs's opinion, and as a result McAdoo immediately set out to find financing to complete the Hudson tunnel. Soon he began to think even bigger—envisioning a great rapid transit network, with electric-powered cars, extending across the Jersey Meadows to Newark, New Jersey to link the many railroad terminals on the Jersey shore with those in New York City. The challenge, as he saw it, was how to build around, through and under the busiest, most densely populated metropolitan area in the country. It was a vision that his newly formed Hudson and Manhattan Railroad would become an important part of.

Work began on completing the old Haskins brick tunnel. In addition, McAdoo's plan called for an underground junction on the New Jersey side, which the second, parallel, tunnel begun by Pearson could not feed into. So that tunnel was abandoned and work also began in 1904 on another tube to the south—parallel to the Haskins tunnel.

Tunneling beneath the Hudson was anything but easy. Rock ledges had to be blasted, and a reef rock formation jutted up 12 feet into the area the tube was to cross. What made this situation especially treacherous was that while blasting had to be done to clear the way for two-thirds of the 18-foot diameter of the tube, the top third was blocked only by silt. If not done carefully, a blowout was sure to occur when the blasts were fired. One such accident did happen on McAdoo's south tube, killing one man and shooting water 40 feet in the air. To protect the lives of the men working inside the tunnel, barges dumped loads of clay on the river bottom at that location to prevent another hole from forming in the mere 15-foot layer of silt above the tunnel. The trick worked and no further blow-outs occurred.

Finally, on March 11, 1904, a little over a year after they began, the workers holed through on the original Haskins tunnel, making the connection with the other half of the tunnel, begun by Pearson, that extended out from the New York shore. Called to the site for the occasion, McAdoo walked through a door in the shield, remarking later that "for the first time in the history of mankind, men had walked on land from New Jersey to New York." The first official train rolled through on Tuesday, February 25, 1908. McAdoo also added two more tubes, from downtown Manhattan, begun in January 1906 and completed in 1909.

By 1910, the Pennsylvania Railroad had added twin tubes running under the Jersey Palisades and the Hudson to the PRR's great new terminal, the Pennsylvania Station in mid-Manhattan. On the New Jersey side, the tracks from the Bergen Hill Portal connected to the Jersey Meadows, which became a hub, known as the Manhattan Transfer, where the switch was made from steam to electricity for trains headed toward the city. Four tunnels also ran from the Pennsylvania Station, beneath the Manhattan streets and under the East River to Long Island. Thanks to a network of tunnels built by individuals with vision and courage, Manhattan at last was thoroughly connected by rail to the surrounding areas.

Tunneling has always meant hard work in cramped spaces—here workers toil on the Lincoln Tunnel beneath the Hudson. Courtesy of Port Authority of New York and New Jersey

William Gibbs McAdoo
The Man Who Pushed Through Under the Hudson

Born in Georgia on October 31, 1863, William Gibbs McAdoo attended the University of Tennessee and became a lawyer in Chattanooga, Tennessee. He soon became interested in transportation, however, and tried to reorganize the street railway system in Knoxville. But this first effort didn't go well—he lost money at it—and before he reached 30 he set out for New York, where he arrived in 1892.

McAdoo was a quiet man said to have "extraordinary gifts." Tall, slender, with bushy eyebrows and deep-set eyes, he possessed intensity, vigor and follow-through. Often thought to resemble Abraham Lincoln, William McAdoo was a finisher, and between 1901 and 1908, he completed the tunnel beneath the Hudson River that no one else had been able to complete.

In 1910, McAdoo's life took another turn when he met Woodrow Wilson, for whose presidential candidacy he campaigned. He served as secretary of the treasury under President Woodrow Wilson from 1912–18, and after McAdoo's wife died in 1912, he married the president's daughter Eleanor Wilson in 1914 in a ceremony in the White House. McAdoo also helped establish the Federal Reserve System, which he was first to chair.

From 1917 to 1919, while the railroads operated under government control during World War I, McAdoo became director general of the railroads for the entire United States. During that time he managed 532 properties with 366,000 miles of track and a paper value of $18 billion. Shipment systems had fallen into a shambles, with thousands of tons of supplies hung up in the wrong places at the wrong times. Calling the freight priority system "devoid of all common sense," McAdoo ordered freight car loadings to be held up until shippers authorized them. The railroads returned to private ownership after the war, in 1920.

At the same time, McAdoo directed several Liberty Bond issues and, in addition to chairmanship of the Federal Reserve Board, served on the Federal Farm Loan Board and the War Finance Corporation.

Thoroughly involved in national politics, McAdoo campaigned for the Democratic presidential nomination in 1920 and 1924, and although he was not nominated, he came very close in 1924, with a convention deadlock between McAdoo and Alfred E. Smith. Finally, on the 103rd ballot, John W. Davis was nominated as a compromise.

Elected senator from the state of California in 1932, he served until 1938, when he resigned. He died in Washington, D.C., on February 1, 1941. His aptly named autobiography, *Crowded Years*, published in 1931, looked back on a life of varied accomplishments, not the least of which had been the completion of "McAdoo's Tunnel."

AT LAST A PERFECT RECORD: THE LINCOLN TUNNEL

The hazards of "air tunneling," as working under increased air pressure was called, were not truly overcome until many years later, with the construction of the third, or South Tube, of the Lincoln Tunnel, completed in 1957. (The first two tubes of this three-tube automobile tunnel were completed in 1937 and 1945—see Chapter 8.) Thanks to improved safety precautions, it was the first tunnel worked under air that had not one single fatality.

Men heading for work on the South Tube wore a badge that read: "Compressed air worker. If this man is stricken on the street send him to the medical lock at 42nd Street and 11th Ave." These tough, burly sandhogs would work 30 minutes under the intense 46 pounds of pressure—enough to hold back 110 feet of water—required for this tunnel. They would then return to the "hog house," where they would lie down, covered with thick clothing to keep warm for at least an hour and rest for another five hours. The day would finish with a 30-minute return bout beneath the water and sludge in the tunnel, described by former construction superintendent-writer Richard W. O'Neill as a "huge steel tube the walls of which looked like a giant waffle iron."

By 1939, two tunnels beneath the Hudson—the Holland and the Lincoln—enabled cars and trucks to drive from New York to New Jersey and back. Courtesy of Port Authority of New York and New Jersey

To enter the tunnel, the men would go into the air lock, an air-tight chamber only 6 feet high with an entrance on each end. Having slammed the door shut behind them, they would sit facing each other, watching for signs of trouble in each other's faces as the pressure rose five pounds. Anyone who became dizzy or queasy at this point had to leave. As the pressure continued to rise, the men would hold their noses and swallow hard or blow their noses to equalize pressure in the inner ear (as people do in airplanes when changing altitudes, and thus, air pressure). Failure to do this, they knew, could cause damage to their hearing, and failure to take seriously any signs of illness and dizziness could result in paralysis or death from the bends.

Once 46 pounds of pressure was reached, the lock tender on that shift would open the door to the tunnel and the men would climb down steel stairs to work in the drenching heat and humidity below. After a half hour of work, their pulses racing in the high pressure, they would leave, with fresh shifts coming in every 15 minutes.

Taking care not to damage the two tubes of the Lincoln Tunnel that were already completed, the work-

ers let the muck into the tunnel through the shield a little at a time. It would thread in, almost like toothpaste, and the men would chop it up into chunks and load it on cars that would carry it out, traveling along a track, through the muck lock.

Tunneling on the South Tube of the Lincoln was by no means an easy job—experience had proved the necessity of the long rest periods to recover from the extreme physical strain these men had to put their bodies under. The work was still back-breaking and dangerous. But at last a major tunnel project had been driven under air with a perfect record—no deaths.

Today, more than a dozen tunnels run beneath New York's waterways—including various pipelines as well as transportation lines built for subways, railroads and highways—making the connections between the great city and surrounding areas. Many of them represent world-famous feats—from the Hudson Tubes in 1908 to the first 2.5-mile Lincoln tube driven in 1937 and the 2.1-mile Brooklyn-Battery Tunnel opened in 1950, both among the longest underwater tunnels in the world. All represented superlative triumphs of human engineering, strength and will against the challenges of nature.

8

GETTING CARS FROM HERE TO THERE: BUILDING TUNNELS FOR ROADS

While railroads continued to be an important transportation network in the United States well into the 20th century, by 1900 Americans had already grown fascinated by a new form of transportation. The "Tin Lizzy" or "horseless carriage," as automobiles or cars were referred to in those days, had many advantages for the average family. They could keep it in the garage and take it anywhere whenever they wanted to, without schedules to meet or tickets to buy. All they had to do was put gas in the tank, and, with those early models, turn the crank on the engine.

By 1916 nearly 250,000 trucks and other commercial vehicles and more than 3 million private cars were registered in the United States. By the following year, the total of registered motor vehicles swelled to 4.8 million, with 435,000 of them trucks. Auto manufacturing was thriving, producing 1.7 million passenger cars—with an average price of $750 per vehicle—and 181,348 commercial vehicles in 1917. Americans had taken to the road.

For tunnelers the automobile brought a new and deadly problem: carbon monoxide. Without effective ventilation, drivers and passengers alike would quickly become asphyxiated in a tunnel of any length. Consequently, the first road and highway tunnels were usually very short. One notable exception to that rule made use of an unusual method to get around the problem.

MITCHELL'S POINT TUNNEL

The Columbia River Highway in Oregon climbs serenely along the south bank of the wide, rugged river, connecting Portland, near the river mouth, with the eastern counties of the state. The region's scenic beauty has always been a major point of pride with Oregonians, and consulting engineer Samuel Christopher Lancaster made a special point of designing the highway to provide travelers with many stunning views along the way.

A rugged ridge of basaltic rock jutted out into the Columbia about 5 miles west of the town of Hood River. It might have forced the highway away from the scenic bank, but John A. Elliott, who was in charge of that section of the highway, told Lancaster, "I believe I have found a place to duplicate the Axenstrasse in Switzerland," a beautiful arcade tunnel cut into the mountains along the shore of Lake Lucerne.

So was born Mitchell's Point Tunnel, also known as Storm Cliff Tunnel, the first major highway tunnel built in the United States. Preliminary surveys showed that building a tunnel had many advantages over running a road around the ridge. A tunnel would be shorter by 1 mile than a road over the ridge and take out the steep 23% grade (rising 23 feet for every 100 feet of road) of the old pioneer wagon road. It would also cost less to build. The 390-foot tunnel would be a rectangle 18 feet wide and 10 feet high, capped by a

Tunnels for Highways and Roads

1870–1985

DATE	TUNNEL	LENGTH
1870	Washington Street Tunnel Beneath the Chicago River in Chicago, the first tunnel built for vehicles in the United States, with two passageways, one for horse-drawn vehicles and the other for foot traffic	1,608 ft. (vehicular tube) 810 ft. (pedestrian tube)
1915	Mitchell's Point Tunnel Alongside the Columbia River in Oregon, the first major highway tunnel in the United States—ventilated with windows	390 ft.
1927	Holland Tunnel First auto tunnel to solve the ventilation problem with a fresh-air system	8,556 ft. (north tube) 8,371 ft. (south tube)
1928	George A. Posey Tube Connecting Oakland, California with the island-city of Alameda. Early use of the immersed-tube method of construction	3,345 ft.
1936	Yerba Buena Tunnel Connects the two parts of the San Francisco–Oakland Bay Bridge through Yerba Buena Island	1,791 ft.
1937, 1954	Waldo Tunnel Built to pass through the Marin headlands and speed traffic flow between San Francisco and Marin County, north of the Golden Gate Bridge. Second bore completed in 1954.	1,000 ft.
1937, 1945, 1957	Lincoln Tunnel Three-tube tunnel beneath the Hudson River, connecting New York and New Jersey	8,216 feet (central tube) 7,482 ft. (north tube) 8,006 ft. (south tube)
1940	Queens Tunnel First road tunnel under the East River, connecting Manhattan and Queens	6,414 ft.
1957	Lehigh Tunnel On the Pennsylvania Turnpike	4,379 ft.
1985	Fort McHenry Tunnel Tunnel in Baltimore, Maryland	1.4 mi.

natural arch with a radius of 9 feet, carved out of the rock. To mark the exact location of the tunnel, survey crews worked along the face of the cliff, dangling from 200-foot ropes. Construction crews began work on the tunnel on March 31, 1915, taking great care in the blasting to preserve the tunnel's most elegant feature: a series of natural arch windows facing out onto the river. The supporting rock around these open win-

dows was left entirely intact, and only a masonry protective railing was added. Ninety feet below, the main line track of the Oregon-Washington Railroad and Navigation Company wound along the edge of the river at the base of the rocky point, and the tree-lined shores of Washington State could be seen on the other side. The natural arch windows of the Mitchell's Point Tunnel had solved the problem of

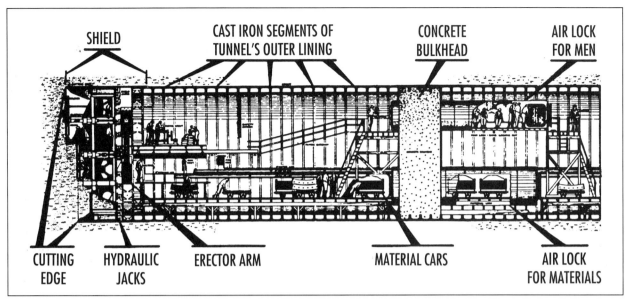

Cutaway view of the Holland Tunnel under construction. Courtesy of Port Authority of New York and New Jersey

ventilation both beautifully and elegantly. But there was one drawback: It was a solution that couldn't be used in many other locations.

CLIFFORD HOLLAND'S SOLUTION

Meanwhile, on the other side of the continent, New York City continued to struggle with its giant transpor-

tation problems—made all the more urgent now by the emergence of the automobile. Cars and trucks lined up daily on both sides of the Hudson River to make their way across by the only means then available: ferry boats.

By this time, tunnels had been driven successfully across both the mighty Hudson and the East River. However, these tunnels were used primarily for

Getting Pure Air into Auto Tunnels

Clifford Holland's solution to the ventilation problem in a tunnel as long as the Holland Tunnel—particularly one for automobiles—was one of his greatest contributions to tunneling. It was based on elaborate theories as well as physiological and mechanical tests conducted mainly by the U.S. Bureau of Mines.

The resulting ventilation system, known as a transverse-flow system, uses huge fans to force fresh air in at roadway level, while drawing off foul air, laden with vehicle exhaust fumes, at the ceiling. Vents throughout the length of the tunnel just above the curb, spaced about 10 to 15 feet apart, deliver the fresh air into the tunnel. The exhaust fans, meanwhile, draw the fumes through openings in the ceiling, into the exhaust duct that runs above the ceiling slab to the ventilation building, where they are discharged through the roof.

Four ventilation buildings, two on each bank of the Hudson River, together house 84 immense fans, 42 intake fans and 42 exhaust fans. These fans, together totaling 6,000 horsepower, are able to make a complete change of the air inside the tunnel every 90 seconds. Air samples from the tunnel are passed through analyzers and monitored constantly so that adjustments can be made in the speed of the ventilation.

Both innovative and effective, Holland's method and principles for tunnel ventilation are still used in many underwater vehicular tunnels throughout the world.

Clifford Milburn Holland

(1883–1924)

By the time Clifford M. Holland was 23, he had graduated as an engineer from Harvard University and had set to work on one of the first East River tunnels. The young engineer once remarked prophetically to a classmate, "I am going into tunnel work and I am going to put a lot more into it than I'll ever be paid for." At 31, Holland was in charge of construction of four subway tunnels under the East River, all being built at once. Even the sandhogs respected his savvy and dedication. "That bird could come down here blindfolded in the dark," one of them once remarked, "and tell us if we was going wrong!" As a newspaper reporter once described him, Holland was a man with considerable presence, "slim-built, with a bronzed face that needs no second glance to tell that its owner knows a great deal about something, even to a stranger who has never heard of tunnel construction."

When Holland was 37, he presented a proposal for an auto tunnel under the Hudson between New York and New Jersey. The two-state commission selected his plan over all others submitted, even over that of the highly respected George Goethals (who had overseen the final construction of the Panama Canal). It would be Holland's greatest project.

After extensive testing and consultation with experts, Holland developed a solution to the biggest problem facing the builder of an underwater tunnel for gasoline-powered vehicles: ventilation. In addition to his engineering ingenuity he brought to the tunnel his tireless attention, remaining on the job, at the works, for almost four years straight, both eating and sleeping there. In the end, the strain destroyed his health.

In October 1924, the tunnel's two headings were drawing finally close, one making its way beneath the Hudson from the Manhattan side, the other from Jersey City. A grand celebration was planned and President Calvin Coolidge was to fire the final blast to join the two by remote control. But when the day finally did arrive, on October 29, it was instead a day of mourning. Two days earlier, Clifford Holland died—having ignored warnings to slow down. He was 41.

Few engineering structures are named after their designers. But as the result of Clifford M. Holland's engineering prowess, vision, calm and constant supervision, and untiring efforts to complete this tunnel, a few weeks after his death his last great project was officially named the Holland Tunnel.

trains and subways and water mains and sewers. City planners were faced with a new challenge: Could an automobile tunnel be built under these same waterways?

The first tunnel for automobiles beneath the Hudson was authorized in 1919 as a joint project of the states of New York and New Jersey. A provision for a toll was included in the proposal to provide the states with a means to maintain it. In 1920, the commission settled on the design proposed by Clifford M. Holland, a young engineer of 37. They appointed Holland chief engineer, and construction began that same year.

Though the big tunnel's two tubes were in themselves a challenge, in many ways the tunneling process was similar to underwater tunnels that had already been built in the previous two decades. The great challenge met by Holland was to design a ventilation system for an underwater tunnel intended for vehicles powered by internal combustion engines.

Holland recruited the aid of experts at Yale University, the University of Illinois and the U.S. Bureau of Mines, and the design he came up with for the Holland Tunnel's ventilation system emerged from a group of exhaustive studies. They ran extensive tests to find out what quantities of gas he would be dealing with. Autos were tested both in closed chambers and on the open road to see how much exhaust they emitted, and what quantities of carbon monoxide and other noxious fumes the exhaust contained. Volun-

The New York/New Jersey state line—under water. The Holland Tunnel opened for traffic in 1927. Courtesy of the Port Authority of New York and New Jersey

teers were also tested to find out the effects of these fumes on people. For a tunnel with a capacity for 2,000 vehicles an hour, it quickly became clear that, given the fact that one-half of one percent of carbon monoxide in the air is lethal, the ventilation system had to be not only effective but fail-safe.

Finally a plan emerged for a "transverse-flow" ventilation system (see box on Getting Pure Air into Auto Tunnels on p. 59). It used a complex of 84 giant fans to push clean air in and draw polluted air out through air ducts running the length of the tunnel. Under normal conditions, only 56 of those fans are needed to keep the air in the Holland free of fumes, with the other 28 kept for back-up in emergencies. This precautionary feature of the system proved its worth on May 13, 1947, when a tank truck loaded with carbon disulfide gas caught fire and exploded in the tunnel. For 500 feet the tunnel ceiling was severely damaged and 23 cars were destroyed in the blast. But the 60 people caught in the

tunnel all escaped alive, despite the poisonous fumes from the fire.

The Holland Tunnel is actually two tunnels, twin tubes pushed through about 60 feet apart beneath the silt of the Hudson, one for westbound traffic, the other for eastbound. They were excavated using shields worked under air pressure. Work on the tunnel began at Canal Street in New York City in October 1920, where a shaft was sunk and the first shield erected. A second heading, from the Jersey City side, was also started heading eastward. Not until two years later, though, on October 26, 1922, was compressed air introduced into the shield chamber to counterbalance the pressure of the water and the actual tunneling began. Behind the compressed-air work area at the tunnel heading, two airlocks provided access—a "man-lock" for the workers and a "muck-lock" for removing materials or muck. Each shield weighed about 400 tons with all its equipment and measured about 30 feet in outside diameter and more than 16

THE STORY OF AMERICA'S TUNNELS

feet long. A hood projected 2.5 feet in front of the shield, while 30 10-inch jacks combined to provide a forward thrust of 6,000 tons.

Crews working behind the shield lined the tunnel using 115,000 tons of curved cast-iron sections and 130,000 cubic yards of concrete. A hydraulic erector on the shield lifted the lining segments into place to form a complete ring. As each section of lining was completed, the hydraulic jacks on the shield were braced against the lining to move the shield forward. When the shield had moved forward the width of one lining ring, new segments were lifted into place and bolted together. Then the whole process would begin again.

The project had its challenges. At one point there were five shields working on twin headings, with connecting drifts. And about a thousand feet of solid rock near the New York shore had to be blasted. Inevitably, given the extremely difficult river bottom conditions, there were accidents. Holland himself was destroyed by the tunnel in a way. Having remained on the site night and day for nearly four years, he died two days before the first breakthrough in 1924. His successor, Milton Freeman, also died suddenly five months later, with the job finally finished under the direction of the project's third chief engineer, Ole Singstad.

When the tunnel was finished, 20,000 people walked through it in the opening day celebration, followed by 51,000 more in cars. The Holland Tunnel was opened to traffic on November 13, 1927. Snaking as deep as 93 feet beneath the water surface, each two-lane roadway is 20 feet wide, while the external diameter of each tube measures 29 feet 6 inches. Operating headroom inside the tunnel, however, is a slightly claustrophobic 12½ feet. Portal to portal, the north tube extends 8,558 feet, while the south tube is 8,371 feet long (roughly a mile and a half). At the time the tubes were completed in 1927, they were the largest in the United States.

Later tunnels in the area—including the Lincoln, the Queens Midtown and the Brooklyn-Battery—as well as many others throughout the world were patterned after its design and construction. For the contribution its engineers made to tunneling design, the Holland was named a National Historic Civil and Mechanical Engineering Landmark in 1984.

Completion of the Holland Tunnel effectively strengthened the economy of both New York and New Jersey, enabling commercial traffic to cross the Hudson River in minutes. Before the tunnel was built the trip by ferry often took hours. Today, nearly 15 million vehicles

a year travel through the tunnel, eastbound alone, from New Jersey to Manhattan. If traffic both ways were counted, the figure would approach 30 million.

MORE OF A GOOD THING: THE LINCOLN TUNNEL

The Holland Tunnel was, in fact, such a success that traffic began to back up at the tunnel entrances. The need for another tunnel across the Hudson soon became clear, and plans were laid for the Lincoln Tunnel, to run from midtown Manhattan to Weehawken, New Jersey on the west bank of the Hudson River.

Begun in May 1934, the first tube of the Lincoln Tunnel was holed through under the river August 2, 1935. It was completed in 1937 and opened for traffic on January 10, 1938. Construction methods for the Lincoln Tunnel, as well as the ventilation system of 56 fans, were very similar to those used for the Holland Tunnel. The outer rim of the tunnel is made of 14 plates, or sections, each weighing 3,330 pounds, with a 700-pound key plate. The two-lane roadway is 21.5 feet wide, with an operating headroom of 13 feet, and the external diameter is 31 feet. Exhaust air ducts run above the roadbed, while fresh air ducts run beneath it.

Once the first tube of the tunnel was in operation, 400 lights on a central control board in the Weehawken ventilation building kept the supervisory operator informed on the status of every part of the electrical and ventilation systems. From here, the operator could also oversee all traffic lights in the tunnel and monitor the amounts of carbon monoxide drawn from the tunnel by the exhaust fans.

Meanwhile, work continued on the North, or second, Tube, which already extended between 1,000 and 1,400 feet from the Weehawken portal, as described by a newspaper reporter at the time:

Some 175 . . . sandhogs, the same who built the bore to be used for present traffic, this very minute are forcing their way through the [north] tube, heading for the great caisson just completed on the New York side of the new project. . . .

The sandhogs, always faced with the dreaded "bends," are working under sixteen to seventeen pounds of air pressure, to be increased as they go further under the river bed. The sandhogs who built the caisson in New York, did so under the terrific pressure of twenty-five pounds.

The second tube, 7,482 feet long, was opened to the north of the original tunnel on February 1, 1945.

Finally, the third or South Tube, 8,006 feet long, was opened on May 25, 1957. The Lincoln Tunnel also is the only three-tube vehicular underwater tunnel in the world. This feature of the tunnel does offer the Port Authority excellent flexibility in handling traffic flow. When the rush hour traffic presses toward Manhattan in the morning, the Port Authority opens two tubes running eastward. In the evening, when the rush reverses, two of the three tubes are opened to the west.

The Port Authority has also shown the tunnel's flexibility in another way. When 19 elephants in the Ringling Bros. & Barnum & Bailey Circus got stranded in New Jersey due to a railroad strike, the Port Authority of New York and New Jersey saw to it that they got to their engagement at Madison Square Garden in New York City. In the middle of the night, these 19 elephants walked from New Jersey to New York through the Lincoln Tunnel on May 18, 1971.

On December 27, 1937, when the first tube opened, the annual traffic flow was expected to be 7 million vehicles. Today, traffic in the Lincoln Tunnel has increased to nearly six times that figure. If all 41,641,305 vehicles that traveled through the Lincoln Tunnel in 1989 were lined up bumper to bumper they would stretch around the earth six times! Some 117,000 vehicles make the trip every weekday, and on weekends the figure climbs to 216,800.

AUTO TUNNELS OPEN UP THE COUNTRY

By the 1930s, all across the nation, communities, counties and states were having to face the challenge of building roads to meet the growing demands of automobiles, buses and trucks. In some cases building those highways also meant cutting tunnels through mountains.

The Yerba Buena tunnel connected the two parts of the Bay Bridge, shown here still under construction. Completed in 1936, the Bay Bridge stretched nearly 8 miles, including approaches and the tunnel. Courtesy of California Department of Transportation

Tunneling begins on Yerba Buena Island (then known as Goat Island) in the San Francisco Bay. Courtesy of California Department of Transportation

Concrete sections were used to reinforce the walls and roof of the Yerba Buena Tunnel. Courtesy of California Department of Transportation

Jumbo traveling on tracks to a tunnel face on the Pennsylvania Turnpike, 1966. Courtesy of William Shank

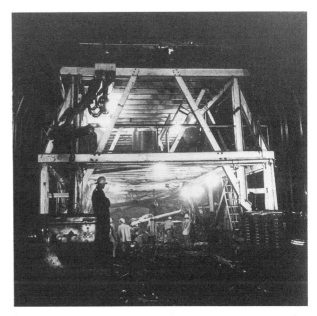

A jumbo at work inside a Pennsylvania Turnpike tunnel. Courtesy of William Shank

In the San Francisco Bay Area, the 1930s saw construction of a great 7-mile bridge across the bay between San Francisco, at the tip of a peninsula, through a short tunnel on Goat Island, later known as Yerba Buena Island, and eastward to Oakland, on the mainland. The tunnel was typical of many highway tunnels—short enough to need no special ventilation system and lined with concrete. When completed, the San Francisco–Oakland Bay Bridge, with its tunnel, served as a much-needed link between these two ports.

In Pennsylvania, the Allegheny Mountains had, since colonial times, presented a major obstacle to the smooth flow of transportation. The Lincoln Highway, built in 1916, crossed over the summits of six of these mountains with grades so steep that many automobiles couldn't make it, especially in bad weather. But a quirk of history provided Pennsylvanians with a unique solution.

During the years from 1883 to 1885, railroad tycoon Cornelius Vanderbilt had begun a giant railroad project that involved driving nine tunnels through the solid rock of the Alleghenies, using pick axe and shovel, compressed air drills and blasting. The South Penn, or "Vanderbilt's Folly," as this railroad project was also known, would have competed heavily with the Pennsylvania Railroad. It potentially offered shorter connections than the older line from Pittsburgh to many important cities such as New York, Philadelphia and Harrisburg. In 1883, construction began simulta-

neously on nine tunnels, as well as the rest of the line, with Robert H. Sayre in charge as chief engineer. Six and half miles of tunnels were hurriedly excavated, and 27 workers lost their lives in the two years of construction, many of them killed as a result of the dangerous blasting and cave-ins in the tunnels.

Vanderbilt, however, was finally convinced by New York financier and banker John Pierpoint Morgan that the type of route duplication and cut-throat competition he was engaged in was destructive to the entire business community. A compromise deal was hammered out between Vanderbilt's New York Central Railroad and the rival Pennsylvania Railroad, and the South Penn was never built.

In 1935, the Pennsylvania State Highway Department and the federal Works Progress Administration cooperated on a project to survey the old South Penn route to see if it could be used for a through highway. In fact, survey teams in 1936 found that six of the nine tunnels originally begun more than 50 years earlier by Vanderbilt's crews were sound enough to be used. Some 70% of the old excavations were in excellent condition, according to their reports, and only 3 miles of tunneling remained to be holed through. "From a geological point of view," explained engineer and transportation historian William Shank, "the 1885 tunnels had been located with uncanny skill in narrow portions of the ridges and at right angles to the strike (or trend) of the rock strata. Thus, the natural struc-

Historical Headlines

1905–1949

1909   The Sixteenth Amendment to the Constitution, granting Congress the power to levy and collect income tax, is sent to the states for ratification.

1912   New Mexico becomes the 47th and Arizona the 48th state. No new states will be admitted until Alaska and Hawaii are admitted to the union in 1958 and 1959 respectively.

1914   World War I breaks out in Europe.

        The United States completes the Panama Canal, originally started by the French 33 years before.

1915   German attacks on U.S. ships threaten U.S. noninvolvement in World War I.

1917   April 2. United States declares war on Germany.

1918   President Wilson presents his 14 Points that he feels are necessary to peace, which are later accepted; the fighting comes to an end.

1919   International peace conference at Versailles.

        Daily airmail service begins between New York City and Chicago.

1920   The Nineteenth Amendment is ratified, granting the right to vote to women.

1921   July 20. World War I is officially declared at an end by Congress and the United States signs and ratifies treaties.

1927   Charles A. Lindbergh flies from New York to Paris solo in his aircraft, *Spirit of St. Louis.*

1929   October. Stock market crashes. The crash is the forerunner to the Great Depression.

        Canalization of the Ohio River is completed.

1930   The economy sags drastically, unemployment approaches 4 million and the Great Depression begins.

1939   Germany invades Poland and World War II begins, although the United States has not yet entered the war.

        Bronx-Whitestone Bridge, over Long Island Sound, is completed.
        First televised baseball game.

1940   Completion and, four months later, the destruction of the Tacoma-Narrows Bridge.

1941   December. After Japan attacks Pearl Harbor, Hawaii, the United States declares war on Japan and enters World War II.

        Scientists begin work on the Manhattan Project, the development of the atomic bomb.

1944   Franklin Delano Roosevelt is reelected president for a fourth term.

1945   Roosevelt dies and Harry S Truman, his vice president, becomes president.

        May 7. Adolf Hitler commits suicide and Germany surrenders.

        The United States drops an atomic bomb on Hiroshima, Japan. About 135,000 deaths and injuries result. The United States drops a second bomb on Nagasaki, and Japan surrenders on August 14.

        U.S. troops enter Korea south of the 38th parallel, replacing the Japanese.

tural strength of the rock was used to best advantage . . ." As planned, the new road would also make use of the grading that had already been done by the railroad crews, greatly reducing the expense of building a highway. And in 1937 a newly formed Pennsylvania Turnpike Commission received authorization to build a high-speed toll highway to extend 160 miles across southern Pennsylvania, with four lanes of traffic, from Middlesex, just west of Harrisburg to Irwin, just east of Pittsburgh. And most of its tunnels, thanks to Vanderbilt's crews and the WPA, were already built!

But when the first section of the Pennsylvania Turnpike was opened in 1940, instead of the estimated 1,300,000 vehicles, nearly twice that many cars and trucks passed through its toll booths that first year. Traffic was soon bottlenecked badly at the two-lane tunnels, often backed up for miles, especially on summer weekends when the traffic was

heaviest. As a result, by the end of the 1960s, new bypasses had been built around many of the old tunnels, while others were double-tunneled, with a second tunnel holed through to relieve the traffic congestion.

With 270,000 passenger cars, trucks and buses traveling the Pennsylvania Turnpike every day by 1988, Pennsylvania's experience with rapidly increasing highway traffic is symptomatic of the crowding that every state in the nation is experiencing today. As a result, many regions are turning to even more dramatic solutions to transportation problems—ranging from intercity transit systems to complex regional and national highway systems. Many of them include huge tunneling projects that make use of ever more innovative advances in technology, not the least of these being those that have been made in immersed-tube underwater tunneling.

9

TUNNELING TODAY: NEW UNDERWATER SHORTCUTS AND RAPID-TRANSIT UNDERGROUNDS

By the middle of the 20th century, automobile traffic had become so congested in urban areas, especially along the East Coast, that the demand for imaginative solutions had become insistent. The wide waterways of the Chesapeake Bay and, on the West Coast, the San Francisco Bay—both of which had once been viewed as transportation assets—now blocked the smooth flow of commuter traffic. A major design change was needed to transform underwater tunneling, so that much longer tunnels beneath bays and wide river mouths could be built. The solution was the "immersed tube."

Also known as the "build-and-sink" method, the immersed tube was invented by an American engineer named W. J. Wilgus, who first used it to build a railroad tunnel under the Detroit River (between Detroit, Michigan and Windsor, Ontario, in Canada) between 1906 and 1910. Fifteen years later, another immersed-tube tunnel was built. This tunnel was an auto tunnel on the West Coast, running under an arm of the San Francisco Bay between Oakland and the naval shipyards on the island of Alameda.

In immersed-tube tunneling, instead of digging under the river bottom, an open trench is dug for the route of the tunnel, using methods similar to the cut-and-cover tunneling technique. Meanwhile, sec-

tions of the tunnel, or "tube," are constructed on dry land and temporarily sealed. They are then towed into place above the trench, where they are weighted down with ballast and sunk. Divers then couple them together on the river or bay bottom.

Built between 1925 and 1928, Alameda, California's George A. Posey Tube (named after its engineer) pioneered the first fully successful use of this method. A single tube, the auto tunnel was constructed of 12 sections each 203 feet long. During construction the tunnel slipped about 6 inches toward the middle of the channel, but the project was saved through the use of jacks, and the tube is still in use today.

The same method was used for the Detroit-Windsor Tunnel, an auto tunnel built beneath the Detroit River between 1928 and 1930. Since that time, as the technology has improved, the immersed tube has become more popular and more widely used. From 1960 to 1964, the immersed-tube technology made possible a long-dreamed-of 17-mile shortcut across the Chesapeake Bay to connect mainland Virginia with the peninsula of land that extends south from Maryland along the eastern coast.

One of the most challenging tunnel projects of the 20th century, the Chesapeake Bay Bridge-Tunnel was

Major Immersed-Tube Tunnels in the United States

1928–1992

DATE	TUNNEL	LENGTH
1928	George A. Posey Tube Connecting Oakland, California with the island-city of Alameda. One of the earliest successful uses of the immersed-tube method of construction	3,545 ft.
1960–64	Chesapeake Bay Bridge-Tunnel A combination bridge-tunnel spanning 17.6 miles, with two immersed-tube tunnels each extending 1,900 feet between artificial islands	1,900 ft. each
1967–74	BART Transbay Tube Links San Francisco and Oakland beneath the San Francisco Bay, at a maximum depth of 135 ft. beneath the surface	3.6 mi.
1988–92	I-664 Tunnel-Bridge Links Newport News, Virginia with Suffolk, Virginia beneath the James River	4,500 ft.

built by an engineer named Percy Michener, who had built numerous bridges, tunnels and railroads in Saudi Arabia. The bridge would allow an unbroken highway route running all the way from Canada to Florida by connecting the eastern shore of Virginia to the rest of the state. This heavily traveled automobile route came to a frustrating slow-down at the mouth of the Chesapeake as traffic lined up to make a long 90-minute ferry ride across the water.

Spanning the 17.6 miles across the bay, though, was a complicated job. The bridge had to be high enough to allow large Navy and commercial ships to pass underneath. In addition the area was a fertile fishing ground. The area to be spanned was actually miles of shallow water, no more than 30 feet deep, with two very deep shipping channels in the middle of the bay. Michener decided not to build over the important navigation channels but to tunnel under them instead. His solution was a complex arrangement of high bridges, artificial islands, long low trestles and tunnels.

Michner's final plan called for first building two artificial islands as entrance and exit points for the mid-bay tunnel. Using dredges he piled sand, gravel, rocks and giant boulders until the islands were built up to 30 feet above the water. And he planned long

trestles to carry the roadway to the islands where traffic would enter and exit the tunnels.

The tunnels themselves were prefabricated, double-walled cylinders built up of 100-foot sections. Built in Texas they were sealed on both ends and towed over 2,000 miles to the Chesapeake Bay. When they reached Norfolk, Virginia the space between the double walls was filled with concrete until the cylinders were partially submerged. Then they were towed to their eventual site where trenches had already been scooped out in the bay bottom. Once on site, more concrete was poured between the walls and they were sunk, guided by divers, into the waiting trenches. At the bottom the ends of each section were cut away and they were linked to form the tunnel. Each of the tunnels was built of 19 sections, welded and sealed tightly against leaks.

The complex, when finished, took traffic first across 3.3 miles of low-level trestles set on hundreds of concrete legs, then down into a mile-long tunnel beneath the bay, up another 3.75 miles of trestle and then down into a second mile-long tunnel. The flow of cars and trucks then emerged out of the second tunnel to cross more than 4 more miles of trestle taking it to a steel-arch bridge. Once over the bridge vehicles passed down a causeway that traversed a mile-

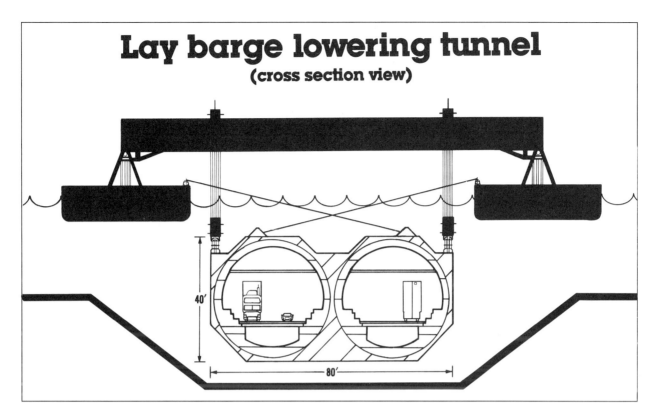

Lay barge lowering tunnel
(cross section view)

40′

80′

In the immersed-tube method, a lay barge lowers ready-made sections of tunnel from the water's surface above. Courtesy of Virginia Department of Transportation

and-a-half-wide island, over another short trestle, another bridge, another short trestle and finally to the opposite shore.

Opening in the spring of 1964, the Chesapeake Bay Bridge-Tunnel cost over $200 million. It was a stiff price, and a complicated project, but the shipping channels remained open, military concerns were successfully met and the travel time across the bay was dramatically cut.

TUNNELING THE SAN FRANCISCO BAY

"General Goethals, Panama Canal Builder, May Solve Transportation Problem by Transbay Tube Project," a *San Francisco Chronicle* headline read optimistically in 1920. The tube would be built, the newspaper story continued, "in order to solve the acute transportation problems facing San Francisco and East Bay communities" such as Oakland, Berkeley and Richmond. But Goethals's visionary proposal, like his plan for what became the Holland Tunnel, was not adopted. However, the position he chose for his tube was prophetic: It was almost exactly the same location where the Bay

Artificial island and cut-and-cover construction at the mouth of the Hampton Roads Bridge-Tunnel in 1973. This artificial island is similar to the ones built for the Chesapeake Bay Bridge-Tunnel. Courtesy of Virginia Department of Transportation

Area Rapid Transit Transbay Tube was actually built 50 years later.

Although completion of the San Francisco–Oakland Bay Bridge in 1936 made travel across the bay comparatively quick and easy, within 10 years the automobile congestion had become so great that in 1947 an Army-Navy commission again brought up the idea of an underwater tube. A two-bore tube, as recommended by the joint commission, would carry electric trains in both directions. It took another 10 years, though, before the California Legislature acted to form a five-county Bay Area Rapid Transit District (from which two of the counties would later withdraw). Two years later seismic studies (to trace the

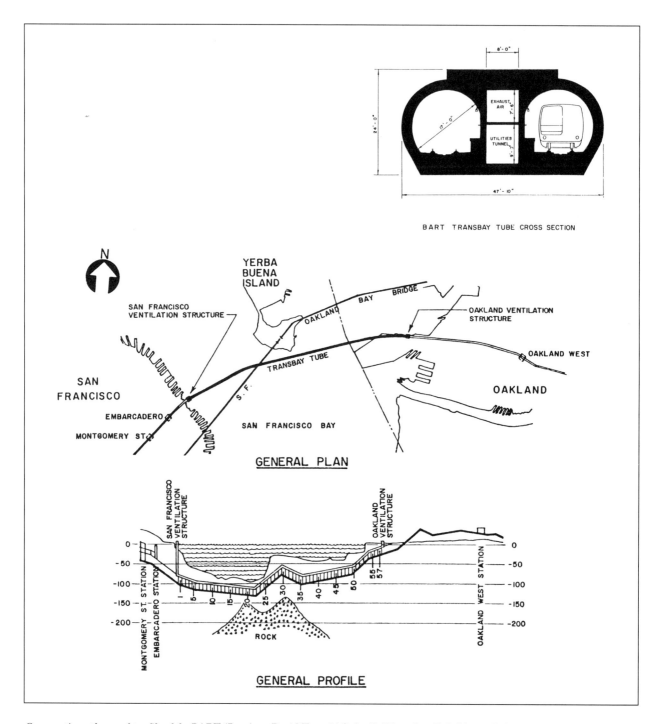

Cross section, plan and profile of the BART (Bay Area Rapid Transit) 3.6-mile "Transbay Tube" beneath the waters of the San Francisco Bay. Courtesy of BART

Two men (near ladder) work on one of BART's huge Transbay Tube sections during its fabrication on dry-land shipways at the Bethlehem shipyards in South San Francisco. Courtesy of BART

possible effect of earthquakes) had begun and the design process was under way. Because the San Francisco area is notoriously prone to earthquakes, designers made special provisions to make the tunnel flexible enough to absorb the shocks of any tremors that might radiate from nearby geologic faults. They decided on flexible connections at both ends—like huge universal joints—to allow the entire tube to move several inches in any direction, and a trench cushioned with soft soil, gravel and mud to protect the tube from jolts. As a result, the "killer quake" of 1989, which collapsed an East Bay section of freeway, destroyed buildings and damaged the Bay Bridge, left the nearby Transbay Tube virtually untouched—even though it crosses under the Bay Bridge.

By the mid-sixties, construction had begun. Like the East Coast immersed tubes, BART's Transbay Tube was built in sections on dry land. Welders set to work on the steel skin, then laced the inside with reinforcing bars for concrete. Each section resembled huge binoculars if you looked at it from the end, with two tubes connected together side by side by an outer skin of steel and a corridor between for pedestrians, ventilation and utilities. Longer than a football field, the sections were 24 feet high and 48 feet wide. Once sealed with watertight bulkheads at each end, each section was launched, like a ship, from the construction site in South San Francisco and towed to a dock in the bay—the first one in February 1967. There, workers poured about 4,200 cubic yards of concrete into the interior (as they also did for each of the 56 subsequent sections) for the track bed and the 2.3-foot-thick interior walls. Now much heavier and barely afloat, each section was towed carefully out

Looking up from the floor of the bay, this artist's conception shows a ready-made BART tunnel section being lowered from the water's surface to its place between two other sealed sections. Courtesy of BART

lion cubic yards of material to cut a ditch 70 to 100 feet deep, with a sloping 60-foot-wide bottom. Because the alignment of the route had to be precise, engineers standing on shore worked round the clock with a laser to guide the dredge barges to the right positions. Just before a section was ready to be lowered, the construction crews added a layer of coarse sand to the bottom of the trench, which then was "planed" to achieve the exact level needed for the tube. The contractor devised a special machine for this purpose, described by one expert as a sort of "floating traveling crane" or big screened barge, which funneled the gravel to the floor of the bay. As soon as possible after the planing was finished, the section was sunk—to avoid disturbance by underwater currents of the carefully arranged trench bottom.

The last of the 57 sections sank into place in April 1969, just two years after the first. It took another four years to complete the inside finishing—including track laying, electrification, and installation of ventilation systems and train control equipment. The first test run was conducted on August 10, 1973, and on September 16, 1974, the BART Transbay Tube opened for business. More than 6,000 people traveled through the tube that day.

In its first 10 years of operation, from 1974 to 1984, passengers through BART's Transbay Tube increased from about 12 million a year to about 28 million. In all, during those 10 years nearly 200 million people traveled beneath the bay.

ACROSS THE JAMES RIVER

The most recent of the big immersed-tube projects, Virginia's I-664 Tunnel, was built using the same principles employed for building the Chesapeake Bay Bridge-Tunnel and the BART Transbay Tube. The design was begun in 1977 for this short-cut across the broad mouth of the James River to connect Newport News, Virginia and Suffolk, Virginia. Overall, the connecting tunnel-bridge link spans 4 miles, with almost a mile of tubing dipping below the water to avoid obstructing the shipping channel. The first island was begun in September 1985, with the first section of tunnel submerged on March 31, 1988. At $126 million, the contract for building the tunnel is the largest ever awarded by the state of Virginia. Built at the Bethlehem Steel shipyard at Sparrows Point, Maryland, the tunnel's 15 steel seg-

into the water to its position. Once positioned, 500 tons of gravel ballast was added to bins on top of each section, sinking it into position in the trench that had been dug on the floor of the bay. Then the divers went to work, aligning the sections and welding them together.

One of the most remarkable innovations of the BART tunnel project was the decision to use steel sections unprotected by concrete from the highly corrosive salt water of the bay. Any protective coating of concrete or paint is bound to develop small holes or flaws, and salt water will seep into any such "cracks in the armor" and destroy the steel beneath. So a system of "cathodic protection" was used instead. Corrosion is actually a type of electrical process, which can be reversed by introducing a counteracting current in the opposite direction. Cathodic protection has been used successfully on buried oil pipes in the deserts of the Middle East and has also worked very well for BART.

Construction of the trench, meanwhile, presented some big challenges. The initial dredging was done by clamshell dredges, removing 5.7 mil-

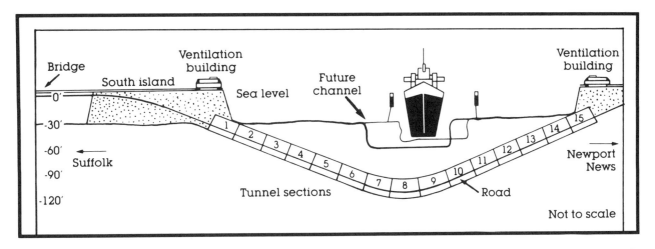

This cutaway view shows how the I-664 tunnel extends in sections beneath the water between two human-made islands. Courtesy of Virginia Department of Transportation

ments are gigantic: 80 feet wide, 40 feet high and 300 feet long, and double-barreled like the BART sections. Each segment, weighing 28,000 tons, contains over 1,150 tons of steel and 10,000 cubic yards of concrete. The completed bridge-tunnel complex opened for traffic in April 1992, greatly alleviating the traffic congestion over the nearby Hampton Roads Bridge-Tunnel.

Lay barge, with tunnel section, floating on the surface of the James River. Courtesy of Virginia Department of Transportation

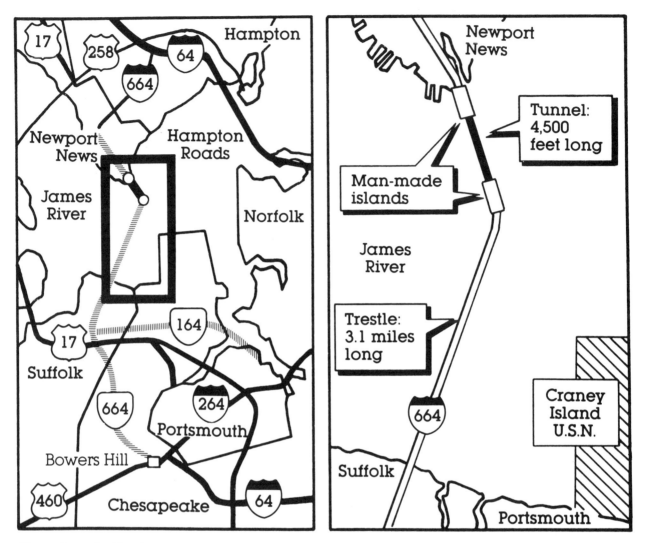

The nearly completed I-664 bridge-tunnel across the James River in Virginia allows traffic to flow directly from Newport News to Suffolk, relieving the traffic congestion on the Hampton Roads Bridge Tunnel, just down river. Courtesy of Virginia Department of Transportation

THE UNDERGROUND ROUTE

Tunnels are so practical and have become so much a part of everyday life that it's easy to take for granted the ingenuity it took to conceive of them and the courage it took to build them. Every day commuters in New York stream beneath the rivers surrounding Manhattan. And thousands of cars head daily through short mountain tunnels in the San Francisco Bay area or cut-and-cover tunnels in Seattle. People forget the great weight of earth and rock or water and silt held back by steel and masonry. And it's easy to overlook the brilliance of inventions that have made these feats of engineering possible—from Burleigh drills to huge immersible tubes, and from the Greathead Shield to giant jumbos.

But as long as the shortest distance between two points is a straight line, people will continue to find better and safer ways to build longer and deeper tunnels—because the shortest straight line often runs underground.

Historical Headlines

1950–1992

1950   New Tacoma-Narrows Bridge (replacing "Galloping Gertie") is completed.

The United States recognizes the new country of Vietnam and sends military advisers to teach the use of weapons.

1951   The Delaware Memorial Bridge across the Delaware River conects New Jersey and Delaware, with a total length of 3.5 miles. (Augmented by a second bridge to accommodate traffic in 1968.)

First transcontinental television broadcast in the United States.

1955   The Tappan Zee Bridge, using several types of spans to cross the Hudson River, is finished at Tarrytown, New York. It boasts the world's heaviest cantilever at the time.

1957   Completion of the Mackinac Bridge across the Mackinac Straits in Michigan.

Soviets launch the first artificial satellite, called *Sputnik*.

1961   In an orbital space flight Soviet cosmonaut Yuri Gagarin becomes the first human in space (April 12). On May 5, in a suborbital flight, Alan Shepard becomes the first American in space.

The United States begins direct military support to South Vietnam, in the form of two helicopter units.

1962   John Glenn becomes first American to make an orbital flight in space.

1963   Civil rights demonstrations throughout the nation. Medgar W. Evers, an official of the NAACP, is shot and killed in Jackson, Mississippi.

President John F. Kennedy is assassinated. His suspected assassin, Lee Harvey Oswald, is murdered by Jack Ruby, a nightclub owner. Vice President Lyndon Baines Johnson becomes president.

1964   Reports of North Vietnamese attacks on U.S. gunboats in the Gulf of Tonkin form the basis for U.S. expanded involvement in the war in Vietnam.

A 17.6-mile highway ocean crossing, the Chesapeake Bay Bridge-Tunnel, is completed.

Completion in November of the Verrazano-Narrows Bridge between Brooklyn and Staten Island, New York, the longest suspension span in North America.

1965   The United States sends troops to Vietnam.

Antiwar demonstrations and civil rights demonstrations take place.

1966   The U.S. Department of Transportation established at cabinet level.

This year 78 million passenger cars and 16 million trucks and buses are registered.

1968   The United States and Vietnam hold peace talks in Paris and the United States ends bombing in North Vietnam.

Martin Luther King, Jr., black civil rights leader, is asassinated.

Senator Robert F. Kennedy is assassinated in Los Angeles.

1969   Neil Armstrong and Buzz Aldrin become the first men on the Moon.

1970   Paris peace talks between the United States and Vietnam continue, with increased public pressure to end the war.

1973	The United States and South Vietnam sign cease-fire with North Vietnam; the Vietnam war ends.
1974	Richard Nixon, plagued by the Watergate scandal, resigns as president of the United States.
1976	Gasoline shortages during winter months reduce use of automobiles.
	World's longest nonstop commercial airline flight made by Pan American, 8,088 miles in 13 hours, 31 minutes.
1977	Energy crisis continues in the United States.
1978	New Panama Canal treaties ratified, giving control of the canal to Panama at the end of 1999 and the United States the right to defend the canal's neutrality.
1979	The United States suspends Iranian oil imports in response to holding of 50 American hostages in Iran; energy crunch continues.
1980	U.S. population reaches over 226,500,000.
1981	U.S. hostages in Iran are released.
	About 13,000 air traffic controllers go on strike.
1981–82	Recession in the United States.
1983	October. U.S. troops land in Grenada, intervening in a coup there.
	Thousands of independent truckers go on strike in protest against increased fuel taxes.
1986	The United States launches nighttime air attacks against Libya in a tense stand-off.
1989	Earthquakes in San Francisco severely damage San Francisco–Oakland Bay Bridge and freeway in Oakland.
	East Germany tears down the Berlin Wall, ending the "Cold War" period of antagonism and non-cooperation between the Soviet Bloc and the West (including the United States).
1990	Iraq invades Kuwait, causing another hike in gasoline and oil consumer prices in the United States.
1991	Iraq is driven out of Kuwait by U.S.-led multinational coalition.
	Unsuccessful coup in Moscow reveals weakness in Communist party and central government, leading many Soviet republics to declare independence.
1992	Jury finds police officers not guilty of brutality in the Rodney King case, sparking riots in Los Angeles and other U.S. cities.

APPENDIX

Major Tunnels in America

DATE	TUNNEL	LENGTH
1821	Schuylkill Navigation Tunnel The first U.S. tunnel, begun in 1818; located near Auburn on the Schuylkill Navigation Canal in Pennsylvania	450 ft.
1826	Lebanon Tunnel On the Union Canal near Lebanon, Pennsylvania, begun in 1824	729 ft.
1830	Western Division Canal Tunnel The third tunnel built for any purpose in the United States; enabled the Western Division of Pennsylvania's "Main Line" system to avoid a meandering loop of the Conemaugh River east of Tunnelton, Pennsylvania	850 ft.
1832	Grant's Hill Tunnel At Pittsburgh on the canal extension of the Pennsylvania "Main Line" from the Allegheny River to the Monongahela River; used mostly as a spillway because the connection from the river to the Chesapeake and Ohio Canal was never completed	810 ft.
1833	Allegheny Portage Tunnel (Staple Bend Tunnel) Begun in 1831, near Johnstown, Pennsylvania, for the Allegheny Portage Railroad; first railroad tunnel in the United States (combined railroad and canal tunnel)	901 ft.
1870	Washington Street Tunnel Beneath the Chicago River in Chicago, the first tunnel built for vehicles in the United States, with two passageways, one for horse-drawn vehicles and the other for foot traffic	1,608 ft. (vehicular tube) 810 ft. (pedestrian tube)
1876	Hoosac Tunnel Tunnel on the Troy and Greenfield Railroad in Massachusetts to complete the link between Troy, New York, and north central Massachusetts	4.5 mi.
1890	Grand Trunk Tunnel Beneath the St. Claire River between Sarnia, Ontario in Canada and Port Huron, Michigan. First underwater railroad tunnel in America, built for the Grand Trunk Railroad	1 mi.
1900	Cascade Tunnel (first tunnel) Built for the Great Northern Railroad in Washington State and used by steam engines until 1909, when the railroad switched to electric locomotives to avoid ventilation problems	7.75 mi.

1904	East Boston Tunnel Enabled trolley cars to travel from Maverick Square in East Boston under the harbor to the Court Street station in Boston	1.4 mi.
1908	The Hudson Tubes Begun in 1874 between New Jersey and Manhattan, the first major con- struction project to use compressed air (Hudson & Manhattan Railroad)	5,650 ft.
1910	Pennsy East River Tubes The Long Island Railroad begins service from Manhattan under the East River	14,172 ft.
	Pennsylvania Railroad New York Tunnel Extension Extends PRR service from New Jersey to Manhattan beneath the Hud- son River	15,600 ft.
1927	Holland Tunnel First auto tunnel to solve the ventilation problem with a fresh-air system	8,556 ft. (north tube) 8,371 ft. (south tube)
1928	Moffat Tunnel In Colorado, begun in 1923 for the Denver and Rio Grande Western Railway; 9,000 feet above sea level	6.2 mi.
	George A. Posey Tube Connecting Oakland, California, with the island city of Alameda. Early use of the immersed-tube method of construction	3,345 ft.
1929	Cascade Tunnel (second tunnel) Built by the Great Northern Railroad in Washington State; begun in 1924, it is still the longest rail tunnel in North America	7.75 mi.
1937, *1945,* *1957*	Lincoln Tunnel Three-tube tunnel beneath the Hudson River, connecting New York and New Jersey	8,216 ft. (central tube) 7,482 ft. (north tube) 8,006 ft. (south tube)
1940	Queens Tunnel First road tunnel under the East River, connecting Manhattan and Queens	6,414 ft.
1941	Bankhead Tunnel Crosses beneath the Mobile River in Mobile, Alabama	3,109 ft.
1950	Brooklyn-Battery Tunnel Connects Brooklyn with Lower Manhattan beneath the East River	9,117 ft.
1957	Baltimore Harbor Tunnel In Maryland, beneath Baltimore Harbor, one of the world's longest twin-tube underwater tunnels	7,650 ft.
1964	Chesapeake Bay Bridge-Tunnel Combination bridge-tunnel across the Chesapeake Bay at Norfolk, Virginia	1,900 ft.
1974	BART Transbay Tube Begun in 1967, the Transbay Tube links San Francisco and Oakland be- neath the San Francisco Bay, at a maximum depth of 135 ft. beneath the surface	3.6 mi.
1992	I-664 Tunnel-Bridge Tunnels Links Newport News, Virginia with Suffolk beneath the mouth of the James River	4,500 ft.

GLOSSARY

bends A disease, often fatal or crippling, caused by excess nitrogen in the bloodstream as a result of transferring too rapidly from high to low air pressure, or visa versa.

bore (n.) A tunnel; or, (v.) To make a hole or tunnel.

cut A passage dug or cut into a hillside for a roadway, canal, railway track and so on. An open cut has no roof or cover.

cut-and-cover A method used for digging tunnels by digging a huge open cut or trench, inserting the tunnel lining in the trench, and then covering the roof with dirt or concrete.

drift Any horizontal tunnel, or a small tunnel connecting two larger tunnels.

excavation A cavity or hole from which material has been cut, dug, blasted or scooped.

face The wall at the end of a tunnel, where the digging takes place.

heading Any small tunnel; often a pilot tunnel driven to mark out the route and provide supply access for a large tunnel.

jumbo A number of drills mounted on a moveable frame for drilling tunnels in rock.

lining An interior structure or wall, often of masonry in the 19th and early 20th centuries, added to strengthen the walls and roof of a tunnel.

pneumatic drill A powerful rock-breaking tool that uses compressed air to drive a sharp metal drill-head in successive bursts against a rock or concrete surface.

pneumatic tube railway A railway on which trains are driven through a tube by the movement of air.

portal The entrance of a tunnel.

sandhog A worker in an underground or underwater construction project, working under compressed air.

shaft A vertical or steeply sloping tunnel, providing access from the surface to a horizontal tunnel bore or other underground excavation. Also, in power tools, a cylindrical rod that transmits power as it rotates.

shield A huge, open-ended frame—now usually a cylinder of steel—used to protect workers from cave-ins while driving a tunnel. Workers use jacks to push the shield forward into the earth; then they can safely remove the earth within the shield. Especially important in underwater and soft-earth tunneling.

shoofly A temporary track around a mountain, usually very steep, built to keep traffic moving while a railroad tunnel is being completed.

switchback A zigzag road or set of tracks that enables a vehicle or train to climb a steep hill. Turns on switchbacks are often so tight that a locomotive can't make the turn and requires a switch at each turn, alternately moving forward onto a switch, backing up the next stretch of track and onto the switch at the next turn, continuing in reverse along the next stretch of track, and so on.

BIBLIOGRAPHY

Ames, Charles Edgar. *Pioneering the Union Pacific: A Reappraisal of the Builders of the Railroad.* New York: Appleton-Century-Crofts, 1969.

Beal, Merrill D. *Intermountain Railroads: Standard and Narrow Gauge.* Caldwell, ID: Caxton, 1962.

Beaver, Patrick. *A History of Tunnels.* Secaucus, NJ: Citadel, 1973.

Berkman, Pamela, ed. *The History of the Atchison, Topeka & Santa Fe.* Greenwich, CT: Bonanza, 1988.

Bobrick, Benson. *Labyrinths of Iron; A History of the World's Subways.* New York: Newsweek Books, 1982.

Botkin, B.A., and Alvin F. Harlow, eds. *A Treasury of Railroad Folklore.* New York: Bonanza Books, 1989.

Bowman, Hank Wieand. *Pioneer Railroads.* New York: Arco, 1954.

Bruchey, Stuart. *The Wealth of the Nation: An Economic History of the United States.* New York: Harper & Row, 1988.

Chamberlain, John. *The Enterprising Americans: A Business History of the United States.* New York: Harper & Row, 1963.

Clarke, Donald, ed. *The Encyclopedia of How It's Built.* New York: A&W Publishers, 1979.

Cudahy, Brian J. *Rails Under the Mighty Hudson: The Story of the Hudson Tubes, the Pennsy Tunnels and Manhattan Transfer.* Brattleboro, VT: The Stephen Greene Press, 1975.

Dunbar, Seymour. *A History of Travel in America.* New York: Tudor Publishing Co., 1937.

Galloway, John Debo. *The First Transcontinental Railroad.* New York: Dorset Press, 1989.

Garraty, John A. *The American Nation: A History of the United States to 1877,* Vol. 1, 5th ed. New York: Harper, 1983.

Gies, Joseph. *Adventure Underground: The Story of the World's Great Tunnels.* Garden City, NY: Doubleday, 1962.

Gies, Joseph, and Frances Gies. *The Ingenious Yankees.* New York: Thomas Y. Crowell, 1976.

Groner, Alex. *American Business and Industry.* New York: American Heritage, 1972.

Harlow, Alvin F., with an introduction by William H. Shank. *When Horses Pulled Boats: A Story of Early Canals.* York, PA: American Canal and Transportation Center, 1987.

Heyn, Ernest V. *Fire of Genius: Inventors of the Past Century.* Garden City, NY: Doubleday, 1976.

Holbrook, Stewart H. *The Story of American Railroads.* New York: American Legacy Press, 1947.

————. *The Yankee Exodus.* New York: Macmillan, 1950.

Hollingsworth, Brian. *The Illustrated Encyclopedia of the World's Steam Passenger Locomotives: A Technical Directory of Major International Express Train Engines from the 1820s to the Present Day.* New York: Crescent Books, 1962.

Hubbard, Freeman. *Encyclopedia of North American Railroading: 150 Years of Railroading in the United States and Canada.* New York: McGraw-Hill, 1981.

The Illustrated Encyclopedia of Science and Technology. New York: Exeter Books, 1979.

Jacobs, David and Anthony E. Neville. *Bridges, Canals & Tunnels: The Engineering Conquest of America*. New York: American Heritage, 1968.

Jacobs, Timothy. *The History of the Pennsylvania Railroad*. Greenwich, CT: Bonanza, 1988.

Jensen, Oliver. *The American Heritage History of Railroads in America*. New York: American Heritage, 1975.

Klein, Aaron E. *The History of the New York Central System*. Greenwich, CT: Bonanza, 1985.

Langdon, William Chauncy. *Everyday Things in American Life, 1776–1876*. New York: Charles Scribner's Sons, 1941.

Lingeman, Richard. *Small Town America*. New York: G. P. Putnam's Sons, 1980.

Merk, Frederick. *History of the Westward Movement*. New York: Alfred A. Knopf, 1978.

Meyer, Balthasar Henry. *History of Transportation in the United States before 1860*. Washington, DC: Carnegie Institution, 1948.

Miller, Douglas T. *Then Was the Future: The North in the Age of Jackson, 1815–1860*. The Living History Library, John Anthony Scott, gen. ed. New York: Alfred A. Knopf, 1973.

Mills, Ev, ed. *Overland Route: Lake Tahoe Line*. North Highlands, CA: History West, 1981.

Morison, Samuel Eliot, Henry Steele Commager and William E. Leuchtenburg. *The Growth of the American Republic*, Vol. 1. New York: Oxford University Press, 1980.

Nock, O. S. *Underground Railways of the World*. New York: St. Martin's Press, 1973.

O'Neill, Richard W. *High Steel, Hard Rock and Deep Water: The Exciting World of Construction*. New York: The Macmillan Company, 1965.

Patton, Phil. *Open Road: A Celebration of the American Highway*. New York: Simon & Schuster, 1986.

Plowden, David. *Bridges: The Spans of North America*. New York: W. W. Norton & Co., 1974.

Ringwalt, J. L. *Development of Transportation Systems in the United States*. New York: Johnson Reprint, 1966.

Sandstrom, Gösta. *Tunnels: A History of Man's Quest for Passage Through the Earth from Ancient Egyptian Rock Temples to the Tunnel under the English Channel*. New York: Holt, Rinehart and Winston, 1963.

Schlesinger, Arthur M., Jr., Editor. *The Almanac of American History*. New York: G. P. Putnam's Sons, 1983.

Shank, William H., P.E. *Three Hundred Years with the Pennsylvania Traveler*. York, PA: American Canal and Transportation Center, 1976.

———. *Vanderbilt's Folly: A History of the Pennsylvania Turnpike*. York, PA: American Canal and Transportation Center, 1989.

Shaughnessy, Jim. *Delaware & Hudson*. Berkeley, CA: Howell-North Books, 1967.

Smelser, Marshall, and Joan R. Gundersen. *American History at a Glance*, 4th Ed. New York: Harper & Row, 1978.

Smith, Page. *The Shaping of America: A People's History of the Young Republic*. New York: McGraw-Hill, 1980.

Urdang, Laurence, ed. *The Timetables of American History*. New York: Simon & Schuster, 1981.

Williams, John Hoyt. *A Great and Shining Road: The Epic Story of the Transcontinental Railroad*. New York: Times Books, 1988.

Yenne, Bill. *The History of the Southern Pacific*. Greenwich, CT: Bonanza, 1985.

INDEX

Italic numbers indicate illustrations.